YOU CAN'T MAKE THIS STUFF UP

In Miami it is illegal for men to be seen in public in any kind of strapless gown.

Corvallis, Oregon, forbids young ladies from drinking coffee after 6 P.M.

Moose may not be fed any kind of alcoholic beverage in Fairbanks, Alaska.

Unmarried women in Florida are bound by law not to parachute on the Sabbath.

In Memphis, Tennessee, frogs may not croak after 11 P.M., no matter what.

For hundreds more, look inside LOONY LAWS.

LOONY LAWS

That You Never Knew You Were Breaking

Robert Wayne Pelton

IVY BOOKS • NEW YORK

Ivy Books
Published by Ballantine Books
Copyright © 1990 by Robert Wayne Pelton

Library of Congress Catalog Card Number: 89-77854

ISBN 0-8041-0744-0

This edition published by arrangement with Walker and Company.

Manufactured in the United States of America

First Ballantine Books Edition: August 1991

Contents

Preface

"Laws too gentle are seldom observed; too severe, seldom executed." BENJAMIN FRANKLIN

Roy Bean, the tough "hangin' " judge of the Old West, was fond of telling the story of a "smart alecky" young attorney who found himself pleading a case in the small Texas town of Sweetwater. After the lawyer's long and learned peroration, Judge Bean swept the counsel's arguments aside with a peremptory wave of his gnarled hand. "What you say may well be in all them there law books, all right," snapped Bean, "but it sure as heck ain't the law in Sweetwater."

I have found that most towns and cities throughout the United States as well as all other regions of the world harbor something akin to "the law of Sweetwater" in their statute books. Some bizarre piece of legislation always seems to bear out Charles Dickens' observation: "The law is an ass, an idiot." No one knows how they got there. And certainly no one within living memory has been arrested under most of them. As a matter of fact, officials in some of the areas cited expressed astonishment when told these laws still existed in their respective communities. But there they are, eloquent testimonies to some poor judge's exasperation at having to wade through a daily load of weighty issues for which, in a judicial system dictated by the law of precedents—no precedents existed.

How else can we account for the origins of a law on the books, for example, making it illegal for a woman attired in a bathing suit to go outside without a club? Or an ordinance prohibiting male citizens from "tempting any man's wife"? Or the fact that in one community, people aren't allowed to "hollar snake" in public places?

Carefully consider this Ashland, Kentucky, compilation of ridiculous legalistic verbage. Judge it for yourself. "No person shall knowingly keep or harbor at his or her house within the city any women of ill-repute, lewd character or a common prostitute—other than wife, mother, or sister."

Community leaders in Jacksonville, Illinois, seem to have known how to keep the noise level down. They passed this ordinance way back in 1884: "No person shall halloo, shout, bawl, scream, use profane language, dance, sing, whoop, quarrel, or make any unusual noise or sound in any house in such manner as to disturb the peace and quiet of the neighborhood."

Ottumwa, Iowa (Municipal Code): "It is unlawful for any male person, within the corporate limits of the City of Ottumwa, to wink at any female person with whom he is unacquainted."

Introducing
Loony Laws

LOCAL OFFICIALS WHO wrote some of the old (and sometimes newer) laws appear to have acted for no greater purpose than a good belly laugh. For example, politicos in Kentucky once passed this measure: "No female shall appear in a bathing suit on any highway within this state unless she be escorted by at least two officers or unless she be armed with a club." This amendment was soon after added to the original legislation: "The provisions of this statute shall not apply to females weighing less than 90 pounds nor exceeding 200 pounds nor shall it apply to female horses."

A number of other offbeat pieces of loony legislation were obviously passed in jest. Various lawmakers do sometimes have a marvelous sense of humor. Try this one from the great state of Texas, which has long been noted for its unusual laws: "When two railroad trains meet at a crossing, each shall stop and neither shall proceed until the other has passed." Huh?

And nothing Texans ever do is likely to surpass the resolution they passed that was designed to honor Albert DeSalvo. He was better known as the Boston strangler, the man who allegedly murdered thirteen women. Here it is: "This compassionate gentleman's dedication and devotion to his work has enabled the weak and lonely throughout the nation to achieve and maintain a new degree of concern for their future. He has been officially recognized by the state of Massachusetts for his noted activities and unconventional techniques involving population control and applied psychology."

There are logical reasons for many of the older statutes. Those regarding clothing and women were largely passed in the late 1800s and early 1900s. Such laws were always designed by men who were often quite prejudiced in their thinking by today's standards toward what was then considered "the weaker sex."

Colorado appears to be a hotbed of loony legalese. Their state statutes clearly proclaim: "No maternity hospital shall receive an infant without its mother, except in cases of emergency." So much for bright legislators!

For example, here's an antique 1898 fashion law from Secaucus, New Jersey: "Any person who shall wear in a public place any device or thing attached to her head, hair, headgear or hat, which device or thing is capable of lacerating the flesh of any other person with whom it may come in contact and which is not sufficiently guarded against the possibility of so doing, shall be adjudged a disorderly person."

And women aren't allowed on the streets of Charlotte, North Carolina, in shorts, a bathing suit, or even an ordinary dress. The law states that all females must at all times have their body covered by "a minimum of 16 yards of cloth."

Perhaps the same mind-set that governs the above Charlotte politicos also governs their counterparts in West Bengal, India. No movies showing the act of kissing can be shown in the theaters of West Bengal. Nor can films with kissing scenes be made in that area of the world. Why kissless films? The Minister of Education has deemed that screen kisses "might cause grave harm to society, as they would act as a brain softener."

Consider this old Jasper, Alabama, law regarding wife beating: "Since the Jasper husband is accountable for his wife's misbehavior, he has the legal right to chastise her with a stick no larger around than his thumb."

Laws having to do with Sunday were usually written and passed as the need arose—with the primary intent to simply keep the Sabbath holy. And the extremely fundamental attitudes of many small-town religious leaders usually prevailed. The church had enormous influence on laws pertaining to a multitude of things.

For example, a blue law designed to prevent "immorality" was passed many years ago in Winchester, Massachusetts. It reads: "A young lady cannot be employed to dance on a tightrope, except in church." And in Memphis, Tennessee, no one is allowed to "sell teddy bears on the Sabbath." While in Pennsylvania, a forty-cent fine can be levied against anyone heard "cursing" on Sunday. If "God" is mentioned in the profanity, the fine is automatically raised to sixty-five cents!

A multitude of loony laws do not read as they were meant to when initially passed. Dogs appear to have it made in pretty little Belvedere, California. They have a misworded ordinance clearly stating: ***"No dog shall***

be in a public place without its master on a leash.''
So much for who's the boss in Belvedere!

Then, almost as if they were participating in a *Can You Top This?* program, Arvada, Colorado, goes one better with their weird no-nonsense canine ordinance: ''If a stray pet is not claimed within twenty-four hours, the owner will be destroyed.'' Huh?

Oklahoma has this wonderful piece of ludicrous legalese to wade through. It reads: ''The driver of any vehicle involved in an accident resulting in death shall immediately stop and give his name and address to the person struck.''

One of the strangest old driving laws still found on

the books is this one from Pennsylvania. It reads: "Any motorist driving along a country road at night must stop every mile and send up a rocket signal, wait 10 minutes for the road to be cleared of livestock, and then continue." Further the statute declares: "Any motorist who sights a team of horses coming towards him must pull well off the road, cover his car with a blanket or canvas that blends with the countryside, and let the horses pass. If the horses appear skittish, the motorist must take his car apart, piece by piece, and hide it under the nearest bushes."

An antebellum piece of legislation in Mississippi still allows servants to be legally killed by their owner. Is it any wonder that decent help is so difficult to find in the Magnolia State? The old statute reads: "The killing of any human being by the act, procurement or omission of another shall be excusable when committed by accident and misfortune in lawfully correcting . . . a servant."

These are merely a few of the situations covered by oddball laws throughout the United States and other parts of the world. Most of these decrees were passed many years ago. Such zany legislation was written and then quickly forgotten with the swift passage of time. All were, at one time or another, passed by intelligent people—many of them attorneys! Most are somewhat biased—they are obviously based upon the personal prejudices of the lawmakers. All are rather humorous. Many are downright strange! And, elected officials in the cited communities had a direct hand in passing each and every one of them. Doesn't this make you wonder just a little bit? But relevant or ridiculous, these statutes are still around—unless they've been repealed indirectly by blanket or collective legislation.

Most of these strange laws were obtained from friends, associates, attorneys, and people met in passing while I traveled around the country. Many other legal oddities have been patiently assembled during my excursions throughout the world. Over the years, I have come to realize that whenever anyone feels inclined to say, "There oughta be a law," there probably already is one, somewhere!

Loony Liberation
Legislation

AN ODD LAW in Cleveland, Ohio, prohibits women from wearing patent leather shoes in public. The city ordinance explicitly states that men "might look" down at the pavement and see the reflection of the woman's legs if she were to appear in public wearing this kind of high-gloss footwear! And through this simple activity, a man "might see something he shouldn't."

How about the various strange stocking laws? Dennison, Texas, allows no stocking adjustments to be made in a public place or on the city streets. Any woman caught performing this "lurid act" can be sentenced to up to twelve months in the state penitentiary.

Bristol, Tennessee, has a similar statute on the books. It simply outlaws a woman from stopping on any street in order to adjust, straighten, or pull up her stockings.

Don't go to Indiana if you are a woman who would like to meet and then start dating a skating instructor. It's a felony in this state for any skating teacher to attempt to seduce a female student. The same holds true in Ohio.

Females who are single, divorced, or widowed must be on guard when going to visit friends in the Orange Juice State. Florida passed a special law that bans unmarried women from parachuting on the Sabbath. Any unmarried woman who does this is subject to arrest, fine, and/or jailing. There is no mention made about unmarried men who might parachute on a Sunday.

And try to stay away from the tiny community of Corvallis, Oregon, if you happen to enjoy a good cup of coffee. There's a strict curfew for women. "Young ladies" are expressly forbidden to drink any coffee after the hour of 6 P.M.

New York City has a tough measure that cuts down on a woman's opportunities to meet members of the opposite sex. *A fine of twenty-five dollars can be levied for flirting. This old law specifically prohibits men from turning around on any city street and looking "at a woman in* that *way." A second conviction for a crime of this magnitude calls for the violating male to be forced to wear a "pair of horse-blinders" wherever and whenever he goes outside for a stroll.*

Monmouth, Oregon, may also turn out to be a drag when it comes to making out. Women who are unchaperoned aren't ever allowed to climb into a car with a man, even if the man happens to be someone they know quite well.

Planning on going shopping in Seattle, Washington, and riding on the transit bus? You'll have to be careful if the bus happens to be crowded and there are no empty seats. No female is allowed to ride on a bus or train while sitting upon a man's lap—unless, that is, a pillow is first placed between them. The possible jail sentence

for a female who violates this law? An automatic six months (the man involved isn't prosecuted).

It is considered a felony in Montana if a wife takes it upon herself to open and read her hubby's mail. The law still is applicable even when the woman is suspicious that he may be playing around behind her back. But nothing is mentioned in this legislation about the machinations of a nosy husband!

Women fifty years old or older must be constantly on the defensive in South Dakota. Such a female is not allowed to go outside for a walk and then initiate a conversation with a married man if he is over twenty.

The quiet little town of Peacedale, Rhode Island, has a unique antiwomen smoking law. A city ordinance makes it illegal for any female to be given a cigarette by a man. And, in fact, in Fargo, North Dakota, men are even prohibited from smoking cigarettes—although nothing is mentioned about cigars or a pipe—in the presence of a female.

If you are a woman, thirsty after a long day at the office, or simply want to enjoy a few drinks while on a date, don't go into a bar or lounge in Wyoming and expect to order bourbon on the rocks—or anything else for that matter. It's against the law for women to stand or sit within five feet of any bar while taking a drink.

Dayton, Ohio, certainly isn't the place to go if you are out of work, a woman, and want to apply for a bellhopping job. The law bans hiring women as bell-hops; such work is reserved only for males.

The city of Tampa, Florida, has made it legal for a man to go out at any time and collect his wife's weekly earnings. But a woman isn't allowed the same privilege when it comes to hubby's paycheck.

Helena, Montana, has a statute which requires all women, while performing in taverns or nightclubs, to wear "no less than three pounds two ounces of clothing" at all times.

In Arkansas a man can legally beat his wife, with the stipulation that he do this no more than once each month.

In Los Angeles a man can beat his wife with a leather belt or strap. But the belt can't be wider than two inches, unless he has his wife's consent to beat her with a wider strap.

Are you a woman who doesn't mind being tickled with a feather duster? The law in Portland, Maine, declares that you are prohibited from letting a man tickle you under the chin with one of these objects. The law doesn't apply to any other part of the body—so it may turn out to be enjoyable.

Laughable Laws
Concerning Horses

IS YOUR HORSE over one year old? Does it always have on a halter when you take it out? You'd better hope so if you happen to be anywhere in Virginia! They have an old law that prohibits horses from being allowed to run, walk, or even graze in public places—if the horse is not wearing a halter and over the one-year age limit.

If you like to ride or show horses, then Wilbur, Washington, certainly will not appeal to you. This quiet little community has a rather strange law on the books that makes it illegal for a man or a woman to "ride an ugly horse." Can you believe that a three-hundred-dollar fine could be imposed on anyone violating this ordinance? It's a fact!

Litterbugs take heed when riding through the city of Detroit, Michigan. Throwing your banana peelings on any public thoroughfare is prohibited by local law. Why specifically banana skins? Because the city fathers felt that banana peelings might cause injury to horses.

Cowboys must be ever alert when riding into Helena, Montana. The police may be carefully watching where they tie up their horses. It's against the law in Helena to tie your steed to a fireplug within the limits of the town.

A statute in South Carolina outlaws the performing of dental work on a mule or horse to conceal the animal's true age.

Arkansas bans the same kind of dentistry if you plan on doing it in order to fool a prospective purchaser of the mule or the horse.

Ever see a horse with its own personal taillight? If not, you may be able to do just that if you go to the trouble of visiting Berea, Kentucky. *This little community has prohibited horses from being out on the streets and highways at night unless the animal has a "bright red" taillight securely attached to its rump.*

You may be in the mood to go swimming with your horse. The politicians in Norfolk, Virginia, say you can't do this in their famous bay. The waters of Chesapeake Bay are declared out-of-bounds for horsemen. Anyone taking a steed in the water is subject to a fine and possible jail sentence.

You'd better have electricity in the place you keep your horse. South Dakota bans any horse owner from carrying a lighted candle into a stable—no matter what the purpose. Nor can you take a burning stick or anything else with fire attached to it.

In California there is a law that bans animals (and this includes horses) from mating publicly within fifteen hundred feet of any tavern, school, or place of worship. The penalty is stiff: up to six months in prison and/or a five-hundred-dollar fine. The wording of this law doesn't make it clear whether the animal will be pros-

ecuted, or if the owner will be the recipient of the pun-
ishment meted out to offenders.

Speaking of Norfolk, Virginia, again, you'd better not
try feeding your horse on the street within the limits of
this great city. To do so will break an old-time ordinance.

Don't go on vacation and take your horse to Leahy,
Washington, if you feel you are coming down with the

flu or a bad head cold. It's strictly against the law there to blow your nose in public places. Is this old law on the books to help protect the health of the citizens? No! The law declares that blowing one's nose out-of-doors might scare a horse and cause it to panic.

Horses wearing cowbells are not allowed to be seen inside the city limits of Tahoe City, California. A municipal ordinance prohibits such adornment.

But the quiet little community of Willimantic, Connecticut, requires that all horses found in the town after the sun goes down must carry at least one taillight.

Do you own a dancing show horse? Don't bother taking it to Rush Springs, Oklahoma. By a vote of 266 to 181 the town residents approved a new ordinance that prohibits any public or even private dancing of any kind. This includes horses!

Kansas City, Kansas, bans reinless horses. The law states that no one can be allowed to "drive a horse" without tightly holding on to the reins. Disobeying will bring a fine.

Burns, Oregon, allows horses in the town's taverns and night spots—but only after an admission fee is paid for the animal.

Want to shop in Birmingham, Alabama? Be careful where you decide to hitch your horse when entering a store. It's illegal to tie up a horse to any shade tree on a city street.

But Omaha, Nebraska, seems to have best solved the parking problem where horses are concerned. Every home within Omaha's city limits must have a hitching post built out in the front yard, and the post must be made of wood.

Washington, D.C., is extremely protective toward its horse population. The capital has a strict ordinance that prohibits anyone from taking the scissors to a horse's tail. No bobtails anywhere within the boundaries of the District of Columbia!

And if you are daunted by all these restrictions and want to sell your horse, you may have a problem if the prospective buyer is a Native American and the horse is under seven years old. In a little town called Wallis, Oregon, a law prohibits Indians from buying horses under this age.

Loony Household Legislation

BE MIGHTY CAREFUL when you sweep that dirt on the floor while housecleaning in Pittsburgh, Pennsylvania. A special cleaning ordinance bans housewives from hiding dirt and dust under a rug in a dwelling.

California has an old law which says that all housewives are required to "cook" their dust cloths by boiling them after using them for housecleaning chores. Failure to properly boil the rags could possibly get you a fine and even jail time.

A piece of odd legislation in the state of Oregon prohibits citizens from wiping any dishes, whatever the circumstances! The dishes must be left to drip-dry after being washed.

And in the beautiful city of Baltimore, Maryland, where they scrub the front stoops every morning, it's strictly against the law ever to clean a sink! You are not allowed to wash or scrub any sink no matter how dirty or stained it happens to become.

In Los Angeles, California, you cannot bathe two babies in the same tub at the same time. But in Piqua,

Ohio, a local ordinance declares that no one can take a bath before the hour of 10 P.M. And in Jacksonville, Texas, lawmakers have placed what they call a "luxury tax" on all bathtubs purchased for household installation and use.

Been planning on building that new home? Like to have two baths, or perhaps even three? Well, think twice before doing this if you happen to reside in Virginia. An old law bans the putting of bathtubs inside a house. Tubs can only be kept outside, in the yard.

Canton, Ohio, has an old piece of legislation prohibiting the ownership of bathtubs entirely. In Detroit, Michigan, it's against the law for anyone to doze or snooze while in the process of taking a bath. Topeka, Kansas, like Virginia, has outlawed the installation of a bathtub in any home.

An odd Portland, Oregon, law says you can't take a bath or "bathe" without wearing suitable clothing. "Suitable clothing" is that which reaches from the bather's neck to his or her knees and completely covers the body. The law doesn't make it clear whether or not this regulation pertains to bathing at the beach or to taking a bath in a household tub. And to top it off, the city fathers of Barre, Vermont, once made it obligatory for everybody to take at least one bath each week—*on Saturday night*.

In San Francisco, California, you are never allowed to beat a rug on a city sidewalk except between the hours of midnight and 8 A.M. Nor can a homeowner or apartment tenant sweep a carpet during this same time period.

Port Jervis, New York, has an odd law on this same subject. You aren't allowed to spread a carpet or rug on

any city street, even if you do this directly in front of
your house or apartment. And Cleveland, Ohio, citizens are prohibited from either beating or shaking a rug
close to any building occupied by more than one family.

Too hot? Has the air-conditioning broken down in
your home? It's a good thing you don't happen to live
in Pittsburgh, Pennsylvania. A local ordinance forbids
anyone from snoozing in a refrigerator.

Don't try sprinkling your lawn while it's raining if
you reside in Savannah Beach, Georgia. Nor will this
community allow anyone to snore unless the bedroom
windows are closed and securely locked. The same is
true in Cambridge, Massachusetts.

In Philadelphia, Pennsylvania, sprinkling your lawn is okay, even during rainy periods, so long as it is undertaken after the sun sets and before it again rises in the morning.

Speaking again of doing dishes! As it is in Oregon, so it is in Minneapolis, Minnesota. This city also has an old ordinance that prohibits anyone from wiping dishes. And in Kansas it's illegal to stack more than eight dishes in any one pile. But Freeport, Illinois, goes one step further. That community has prohibited its citizens from tossing dishes out of the windows of any upper-story apartment or second story of a house.

What to do with your garbage? Huntington, West Virginia, won't allow a family to share a garbage can with another person, even if the individual lives under the same roof. In St. Louis, Missouri, it's against the law to let garbage collect on your roof or on the roof of a neighbor.

A local ordinance in Savannah, Georgia, bars anyone from tossing garbage cans out of a second-story window! In New Orleans, Louisiana, it's strictly taboo to kick a garbage can. And in Lubbock, Texas, no one is allowed to sleep in a garbage can—even if the can happens to be empty.

In Seattle, Washington, it is illegal to remove the lid from a garbage can without having permission of the owner or the city fathers, while in Asheville, North Carolina, citizens are not allowed to dig through the garbage in a trash can. The law in Montgomery, Alabama, goes even further—you are prohibited from even sitting on a garbage can. And Industry, California, has made it illegal to go through a trash can and remove the scrap cardboard.

How about cleaning the house? It's illegal to shake a feather duster in another person's face in Portland, Oregon. And in San Francisco, California, it's against the law to spray laundered clothing with water spewed out of your mouth.

Laundry day can be a hassle in a lot of places. Nappanee, Indiana, will not allow a housewife to hang her wash on a clothesline that measures longer than fifty inches in length. Nowhere in Nappanee are citizens allowed to hang women's undies on an outside clothesline. The city of Los Angeles, California, prohibits its citizens from hanging feminine lingerie out in the open air during the cold months of winter. And housewives in Scranton, Pennsylvania, must be cautious when hanging *their* lingerie in the backyard. This drying method is allowed only when there is a fence high enough to screen the unmentionables from the curious eyes of passersby or neighbors. Nothing is mentioned in the law regarding men's shorts or undershirts. But don't build the required fence with sharp points on top. Pointed picket fences are outlawed within Scranton's city limits.

Now to the kitchen! Did you know that in Dallas, Texas, it's illegal to have a leaky water faucet in your kitchen? And in the state of Florida it's against the law to offer a job to your neighbor's cook! The cook can't take the offered position even if you are willing to double the person's salary.

In Garfield County, Montana, no one is allowed to draw cartoons or funny faces on their window shades, where the pictures can be seen when the shades are pulled down. And in Pacific Grove, California, an ordinance prohibits citizens from pulling their window shades down after sunset.

Laughable Laws
Concerning Church and
the Sabbath

HOMEOWNERS BEWARE! You aren't allowed to sit on your front porch and read the Sunday paper while church services are being held in Fredericksburg, Virginia.

The state of Virginia still retains the old law that was designed years ago to protect its female population from Indians on the prowl. No married woman is allowed on the streets on the Sabbath unless she is properly "looked after." How? Her mate must follow a maximum of twenty steps behind her at all times. And he is required by law to carry his trusty musket over one shoulder.

Plan on taking the entire day off from all home repairs if you live in Schenectady, New York. This city has a special ordinance that makes it an illegal activity to fill nail holes with putty on the Sabbath. In Passaic, New Jersey, you aren't allowed to prepare your home for painting or to paint your home on a Sunday.

The state of Pennsylvania has a most unusual wedding law: no one is allowed to shoot a gun during or after a wedding ceremony. This law specifically bans the shooting of rifles, cannons, or pistols under these circumstances.

Going to visit friends in South Carolina? Are you planning to attend church while in that state? Then be sure to take along your gun. An old South Carolina law declares that "every law abiding citizen" must carry his gun to church with him. And according to this same law, he isn't "obliged" to leave the gun outside the church upon entering for the service.

No member of the clergy is allowed to tell jokes or even humorous stories from the pulpit during a church service anywhere in Nicholas County, West Virginia. The minister can be legally barred from the church by the local police. And they aren't kidding.

Do you own a horse more than one year old who might need a spiritual lift? Then stay clear of Virginia. There a person is prohibited from taking a horse to a church service or even to an outdoor worship service or a tent meeting. Any violator of this law can actually be fined for "willful negligence" and face a possible jail term.

Have a pet bullfrog? Pennsylvania is where you should live to protect your pet best. No one in the state is allowed to shoot bullfrogs on a Sunday.

It's strictly against the law in Cicero, Illinois, to hum on the streets on the Sabbath. In Hawaii, it is illegal to make a loud noise on Sunday. The state of Maine takes a more moderate approach and prohibits anyone from whistling near a church on Sunday during services.

All children should also be aware of these laws. Marble playing is banned on Sundays in Charlestown, Rhode Island. Alabama doesn't pay much attention to

rolling marbles but does prohibit kids from playing with
dominoes on the Sabbath. Memphis has outlawed a kid's
playing with a yo-yo on Sunday.

*In Chaseville, New York, no man, woman, or child
is allowed to drive a dogcart past a church while services or Sunday school classes are in session.* At those
times a wagon pulled by a goat "in a ridiculous fashion" is also prohibited. And it's illegal in Hartford,
Connecticut, to walk or run down a city street with a
dog in a harness.

Maine doesn't allow its citizens to play the radio on
Sunday if they listen to any kind of variety program,
but other shows are fine. New York City prohibits anyone from mowing a lawn on the Sabbath. Santa Fe,
New Mexico, forbids the same thing. And you can't fish
on Sunday in Salt Lake City, Utah, nor can you give
any fish away on the Sabbath.

In Salem, West Virginia, it's against the law to eat
candy any time during the hour and a half before at-

tending a church service. It's also illegal for anyone to sell candy to a minor during this same time period.

Winona Lake, Wisconsin, has a law that says a person can't eat ice cream while sitting at a counter on Sunday. And no restaurant in Kansas can legally sell a slice of cherry pie topped with ice cream on the Sabbath. This same state forbids its citizens to eat rattlesnake meat in public on Sunday.

A minister or a priest is forbidden to perform a wedding ceremony at a skating rink or inside any theater in Portland, Oregon. And in Tennessee, an old state law levies an automatic ten-dollar fine for hunting on the Sabbath.

Some people in the Appalachia area of the United States like to use live snakes in their church services. This practice is outlawed in Kentucky: "Any person who displays, handles or uses any kind of reptile in connection with any religious service or gathering shall be fined not less than fifty dollars nor more than one hundred dollars."

Limburger cheese can't be sold on Sunday in Houston, Texas. Nor can merchants sell goose liver or rye bread. The selling of buttermilk on the Sabbath is outlawed in Springfield, Missouri. No one is allowed to eat peanuts in church within the state of Massachusetts. And in Columbus, Ohio, cornflakes are not to be sold in stores on a Sunday.

And to top it all off, ministers are forbidden to eat garlic or wild onions before preaching a sermon in the little community of Marion, Oregon. Moreover, ministers can't advertise on billboards in order to get more wedding business in Elkton, Maryland, nor can they use this method for promoting their church services.

Lastly, in West Virginia a bridegroom is never allowed to pay a minister less than one dollar for performing his wedding service.

Loony Household
Pet Legislation

MADISON, WISCONSIN, WILL not allow joint custody of a family pet when a couple divorces. The animal is legally awarded to whoever happens to have possession of it at the time of the initial separation.

In Foxpoint, Wisconsin, a local ordinance prohibits all dogs from acting as though they are "vicious animals." They must not bark profusely, snarl, or make any menacing gestures. In Wananassa, New Jersey, a dog is breaking the law if it is heard to be "crying." And in International Falls, Minnesota, cats are not allowed to chase dogs up telephone poles.

One odd law comes out of Danbury, Connecticut: if a dog gets a neighbor's canine pregnant, the owner of the male dog is held responsible. The penalty? To pay for an abortion if the neighbor chooses to have this done to the pet.

Birmingham, Alabama, has a local ordinance that prohibits citizens from tying a dog to a shade tree— even if the animal expresses a preference for lying in the shade.

And surely you want to be alerted to the weird law in Collingswood, New Jersey: no dog is allowed to bark or howl between the hours of 8:00 P.M. and 6:00 A.M. Would you believe that this law doesn't make it clear whether the dog or its owner can be fined for this misdeed?

Cats are banned from howling after 9:00 P.M. in Columbus, Georgia. But in Pasadena, California, the home of the Rose Bowl, the law simply says that you can't keep an animal that howls at night.

You're in serious trouble with the law if you own more than five cats at a time and live within the city limits of Topeka, Kansas.

In Eastlake, Ohio, it's against the law to "molest a dog." The penalty? A twenty-five-dollar fine and/or ten days in the local clink.

Illegal to educate a household pet? Yes, in Hartford, Connecticut. A local law states that no person can be allowed to teach or try to educate a dog.

If you presently own a cat and then buy a pet bird as well, you will be violating the law in Reed City, Michigan. The ordinance declares that "no cat owner" can keep birds on the same premises. To do so brings a twenty-dollar fine.

Do you see a large group of dogs congregating in one area of your property in Shawnee, Oklahoma? Better check to find out if they have a special city permit signed by the mayor. Three or more dogs must have written permission to meet together on private property.

But cat owners have nothing to worry about if the dogcatcher comes around in Virginia. State law prohibits a dogcatcher from bothering cats while he or she is out looking for canines.

Dogcatchers in Denver, Colorado, are required to post a warning notice in all public places before they are allowed to go out hunting for strays. Wonder if the dogs can read?

Shorewood, Wisconsin, is tough on pet owners. This town has a law that specifies that no more than two dogs or cats can be owned by the same family. And it's strictly against the law in Wallace, Idaho, for any person to sleep in a dog kennel.

The city fathers of Provo, Utah, have passed legislation that bans dogs from the streets after 7:00 P.M. But the law says nothing regarding stray cats or other animals. And in Kentucky dogs have a legal right to fight other dogs, but they are not allowed to attack or bother cats.

The small town of Zion, Illinois, has a special law on the books designed to protect household pets from the hazards of smoking. *It is illegal for anyone to give lighted cigars to dogs, cats, and other domesticated animals kept as pets.*

Madison, Wisconsin, discriminates against dogs. A local law bans all dogs from ''worrying'' squirrels in the park beside the capitol.

Cresskill, New Jersey, has taken drastic measures against prowling felines. Any cat who is let out of the house must be wearing *three* bells in order to warn unsuspecting birds of its approach.

Lubbock, Texas, has an ordinance that clearly tells you what must be done to wild animals you keep as pets. They must all be kept on a leash. Included specifically are bears, tigers, elephants, leopards, wildcats, skunks, and monkeys.

You can't keep certain types of animals in River For-

est, Illinois. Banned as household pets are tigers, bears, lions, wildcats, orangutans, panthers, chimpanzees, and snakes, as well as all other kinds of reptiles.

"Bears and other dangerous animals" can be kept as pets in Moscow, Idaho. But they are prohibited from "running at large on any city street."

Alderson, West Virginia, isn't against the idea of keeping a lion for a household pet. But to keep its occupants safe, the city has passed a law requiring that "no lions shall be allowed to run wild on the streets of this city."

If you were a dog, you might enjoy living in Normal, Oklahoma. There's a law there that stops other people from making ugly faces at a dog. Violators can be arrested, fined, and/or jailed for committing such a dastardly act in public.

A quick look at a few more unique laws pertaining to pets: bats aren't allowed as pets in Stillwater, Missouri. Monkeys can't smoke cigarettes in South Bend, Indiana. Baltimore, Maryland, has made it illegal to give a parrot away or to take a lion to the movies.

Laughable Laws Concerning Clothing and Fashion

NEW YORK CITY still has an old ordinance that bans a woman's walking down the street while wearing "body hugging clothing." A female can be fined twenty-five dollars for going out in public in "clothing which clings to her body."

To men who may be going to a costume ball in Miami, Florida: it's against the law there for men to be seen publicly in any kind of strapless gown.

An odd law still on the books in Phoenix, Arizona, specifies that a male must always be wearing a pair of pants when he decides to come into town.

Get that old Christmas spirit each December? Beware if you just happen to be female and live anywhere in the state of Minnesota. It's illegal for a woman to dress up and try to impersonate Santa on any city street. Violaters can get fined up to twenty-five dollars and/or thirty days in the local jail.

Fond of wearing reds? If anything in your wardrobe is the color red, then you shouldn't try shopping, or even just walking around, in St. Croix, Wisconsin.

Women in this little town are forbidden to wear anything red in public.

It's nice to be conscious and to enjoy wearing the latest in hat styles. But Fargo, North Dakota, may not agree with you. You can be picked up and thrown in jail for wearing a hat while dancing or even attending a function where dancing is taking place.

If you would like to go out for an evening of dining, drinking, and dancing in Norfolk, Virginia, then you should be aware of this old law. You won't find a woman in the place who doesn't wear a corset. At least this is what the law requires. And it's also illegal for a female even to go out to a public dance if she's corsetless. Should she be bold enough to remove her corset before getting out on the dance floor, the place can be closed by the authorities. This law even prohibits a female from making adjustments to her corset while she's dancing, or while she's simply present in a dance hall. The proprietor can have his license revoked for permitting such ''wanton'' activities.

Terre Haute, Indiana, isn't a good place for guys who like to girlwatch on the street corner. They can't evaluate what they see very well, because so little is evident. A local ordinance bans all women from the city streets unless they are wearing a dress no more than two inches above their ankles.

Prepare yourself for trouble if you happen to be in North Dakota and like to go to sleep with your shoes on when you come in dog tired after a long day at the office. It's against the law for people there to lie down and fall asleep without first taking off their shoes or boots.

Women in Branford, Connecticut, are not allowed on

the streets or in the stores unless they are completely covered from their shoulders to their knees.

No person is allowed to be on the streets or in any public place of business in Durango, Colorado, attired in clothing that is considered to be "unbecoming" to his or her sex.

But Utah has gone one step further. That great state has actually legislated the required heel size that must be worn by women in any of the state's communities. By this law's wording, a woman's heel cannot measure more than 1½ inches in height.

Stay away from the Carolinas if your pants have hip pockets! The legislature there once passed a bill that bans hip pockets. Why? Because some of the brighter lawmakers decided a hip pocket would be the perfect place for a man to carry a pint bottle of liquor.

You aren't allowed to wear a bracelet watch on your ankle in Elizabethton, Tennessee. Women in Saco, Missouri, are prohibited from wearing hats that "might frighten timid persons, children, or animals."

Austin, Texas, has a unique city ordinance: a person can't go barefoot without first obtaining a special five-dollar permit. This law would certainly conflict with one in Providence, Rhode Island: women are banned from wearing nylon stockings (no mention is made of panty hose).

Maine has two outstanding laughable laws on the books: No citizen can walk down the streets of any town or city if his or her shoelaces are not properly tied. And no spiked shoes may be worn in public (the law doesn't specify if this prohibition applies to females, males, or both sexes).

Toomsboro, Georgia, retains a law that bans its citizens from going out in public places or on the streets without the covering of a shirt.

And a woman shopping in Tucson, Arizona, must be extremely cautious. She'd better not get caught attired in a pair of men's pants or, for that matter, even in slacks designed for females.

Like to sing? Well don't expect to do this if you are wearing a bathing suit in Sarasota, Florida. It's a violation of the law to sing in any public place while attired in a swimsuit, whether a bikini or a more conservative bathing costume.

In Oxford, Ohio, it's illegal for a woman to strip off her clothing while standing in front of a man's picture. And if you are going to the theater in Memphis, Tennessee, throw away those hatpins. You aren't allowed to wear any. New Jersey also considers hatpins to be highly dangerous; its law bans them from being worn anywhere at all in public.

Everyone should be made aware of the loony hotel law still on the books in Salem, Massachusetts. Travelers and vacationers beware when stopping overnight! No man and woman, even married couples, are allowed to sleep nude in a rented room. The hotel is required by law to loan each guest a "freshly laundered and ironed night shirt."

Other areas of fashion are also covered by some rather odd laws. In Carmel, New York, for example, a man can't go outside while wearing a jacket and pants that do not match perfectly. Massachusetts's law regarding clothing is even stranger: no one is allowed to appear in public while wearing "outer garments" that may leave the arms bare, even on hot summer days.

You may have a friend who shot a wild turkey and

gave you some of its feathers. They won't ornament your attire in Franklin, Massachusetts. The law doesn't allow anyone to wear a turkey feather in a cap or hat. (Wonder what the Pilgrim Fathers would have made of that!)

In Lewes, Delaware, however, the important issue is not hats, but pants or slacks. You can't wear any pants that happen to be "form-fitting" around the waist.

And finally, Silver City, New Mexico, has a law banning women from putting on clothing that would class them as being "dressed partly or entirely as a man."

Loony Sport and
Gambling Legislation

A Tucson, Arizona, statute reads: "It shall be unlawful for any visiting football team or player to carry, convey, tote, kick, throw, pass or otherwise transport or propel any inflated pigskin across the University of Arizona goal line or score a safety within the confines of the City of Tucson, County of Pima, State of Arizona." Violators of this unique football legislation can be given a three-hundred-dollar fine and not less than three months' incarceration in the city jail.

Hawaii is not the place to go if you'd like to race your horse after the sun goes down. The legislature passed a bill that prohibits horse racing at night.

If you happen to be in Richmond, Virginia, having a cup of coffee with a friend, don't flip a coin in order to determine who pays the bill. Richmond has an ordinance that makes it illegal to match coins in any eating establishment to see who ends up paying for a cup of coffee. Nothing in this law mentions tea drinkers!

Tennessee law provides a fine of five hundred dollars or six months in jail for the captain and the engineer in charge of a steamboat who race their boat against another one or attempt to make their boat excel another boat in speed. If the boat's boiler bursts or any of its machinery breaks down and the life of another person is endangered, conviction carries a prison sentence of not less than two years.

McPherson, Kansas, has banned "small boys" from playing marbles. Those who sponsored that statute did so "lest they acquire a taste for gambling." (Nothing is mentioned about little girls, who are presumably immune to such temptation.)

Like a good game of cards now and then? Well, be extremely careful when and with whom you decide to play cards in Globe, Arizona. A city ordinance prohibits the playing of card games on the streets with an American Indian. You'll be put in jail if you disregard this ban.

Wrestlers in California are not allowed to make ugly faces at one another during the course of a public match. This law was passed years ago because legislators believed such facial contortions could often influence the match's outcome.

In Connecticut it's illegal for wrestlers to fight with anything other than their hands and feet. Specifically outlawed are bottles, chairs, and other objects.

New Hampshire retains an old law that penalizes gamblers who lose. They're forbidden to pawn the clothes off their backs in order to pay off a bad gambling debt.

Are you a sports lover who would enjoy seeing a man box a bull? This bout won't ever take place in Washington, D.C., where such sporting events are prohibited by law. Now maybe someone will consider passing legislation in the nation's capital that will make bull *throwing* illegal.

Ohio tops them all when it comes to racing laws! That state says a jackass must not ever be ridden faster than the legal limit of six miles per hour.

If you find yourself entering your pet mule in a race in Texas, resign yourself to the fact that the animal may refuse to leave the starting post. Lighting a fire under the creature might do the trick, but that's illegal in the Lone Star State.

Sulphur, West Virginia, won't allow its citizens to sell their homes in order to obtain "frivolous money for gambling." The state of Maine regulates the amount a gambler can win at one time—the legal maximum is a mere three dollars. Also in Maine, if you are married and lose all of your cash gambling, your wife has the legal right to sue and recover any money you've lost.

Females are banned from entering pool halls in Huntsville, Alabama. Nor can a woman place a bet in a pool hall "while men are in attendance." In Burley, Idaho, the law bans women from playing pool at all in a public pool hall or club.

Thinking of adding something new and exciting to your gambling activities? It can't be done within the city limits of Schulter, Oklahoma. There it's strictly against the law for a woman to participate in any form of gambling or game of chance while in the nude, while dressed in revealing and sheer clothing, or while simply wrapped in a towel. Nothing is mentioned about how men may be attired.

Fort Madison, Iowa, allows absolutely no cardplaying on the streets of the city. And in Fort Smith, Arkansas, even cardplaying in the home on Sundays has been outlawed. New York City's law is strange: it bars all citizens who live within a one-mile radius of an armory from having a deck of cards in their house or apartment.

"Kibitzing," or helping a cardplayer, is prohibited by special statute in Emporia, Kansas. Specifically outlawed is someone's assisting a player in bridge, poker, or solitaire.

Colorado has a unique law regarding the betting of your hard-earned cash on dogfights. It's even illegal to attend a dogfight as a casual observer. Idaho also has a law prohibiting people from inciting dogs to fight and from placing bets on dogs who might be seen fighting in the streets.

Here's another report on glamorous Hawaii. Swimming meets seem to be definitely out, unless perhaps undertaken in the nude! No person, according to this outdated law, can legally be seen in public while attired only in a pair of swim trunks. Surfers may also find themselves in trouble while doing their thing on the beautiful beaches in the Waikiki area.

An old Haverhill, Massachusetts, ordinance bans women from wrestling at public (or even private) functions. City fathers considered such a sport as one that could "undermine the dignity of womanhood."

Gloversville, New York, took a similar stand in passing an ordinance prohibiting wrestling performances by females within the limits of that fair city.

Wrestlers of either sex in Philadelphia, Pennsylvania, can be prosecuted and heavily fined for throwing their opponents out of the ring.

Now on to the prizefights: Sacramento, California, still retains an old measure that bans minors from at-

tending a boxing exhibition in the city. Boxing enthusiasts in Wisconsin can't make remarks during a prizefight anywhere in the state. And whistling and the giving of "cat calls" or "razzberries" to anyone are prohibited in Kentwood, Louisiana. Wichita, Kansas, is strictest of all, though; there you aren't allowed even to see prizefight scenes in movies.

Laughable Laws
Concerning Farming

HERE ARE A few of the old-time laws covering agricultural buying, selling, and trading during the night hours. You can't legally trade horses after dark in rural Franklin, Kentucky. Farmers in Tennessee can't sell and customers aren't allowed to purchase cotton after dark. Raising chickens? You can't buy or sell these birds after sundown in Idaho without permission from the sheriff. Alabama still has an old law that declares that no mules can be traded after supper when the sun has already gone below the horizon.

A unique law in the quiet little town of Oak Park, Illinois, prohibits roosters from crowing before the hour of 6 A.M. And in Lakeland, Florida, all roosters must be kept in a box or a pen where they can't raise their heads high enough to crow!

You are not allowed to throw bales of hay from a second-story window within the city limits of Baltimore, Maryland. But in Montgomery, Alabama, no one can toss hay bales from *any* window in his or her house.

Elkhart, Indiana, farmers cannot feed either horses

or cows on the city sidewalks. Nor can they let their cows and chickens run loose on the streets. And you can't sell a dead hog in Louisiana if it is dressed and the head is not with the body. Even the ears must be left intact.

Here are a few more great laws every farmer worth his salt should know. You can't take your hogs or pigs into a public building within the city limits of St. Paul, Minnesota. No hogs are allowed "to roam loose between March 1 and October 20" in Nottingham, Maryland. You can't have a hog roundup and drive your hogs through the streets of Philadelphia, Pennsylvania. And exclusive Boston, Massachusetts, bans anyone from using the roads for driving Texas cattle if those same roads were formerly used for driving other cattle.

Are you a farmer who needs a little assistance in getting your fields plowed? Then be thankful you're not farming in North Carolina. That state has a special statute regulating the use of elephants on the farm. You may not plow a cotton field with one of these creatures.

Going to sell off some stock to the local meat packing firm? Are you looking forward to butchering a cow and stocking the family freezer? Think twice before you take action in Fayetteville, Arkansas, which has an old law that prevents the killing of "any living creature." Under this strange ordinance, a local citizen had better hope he doesn't ever find roaches in the kitchen.

Would you believe the following? You aren't allowed to pick the feathers from a goose while the bird is still alive and kicking in California. Nor does California let its farm citizens keep chickens, turkeys, goats, cows, and other farm animals in an apartment. And you also can't plant a garden in a California cemetery.

Your horse dead tired after the long ride to town from the farm? Want to make it as comfortable as possible? Then don't take the animal into an apartment and let it sleep in the bathtub in Brooklyn, New York. That New York City borough has an old law that prohibits such activities.

You can't blindfold a bull and take the animal down a public road or highway in Arkansas. In McDonald, Ohio, farmers are not allowed to march a goose down a city street. Fowl, especially roosters, are prohibited from going into bakeries in Massachusetts. And aliens are banned from letting their goats run loose throughout West Virginia (the law doesn't seem to apply to American citizens).

And here are some more goodies: a farmer is not allowed to ride an ox down the street in a "violent manner" if he happens to be in the community of Jefferson City, Missouri. A lawyer may be disbarred in Clarendon, Texas, if he refuses to accept farm products in lieu of payment for his legal fees. Every cow loose on the streets and strolling around Seattle, Washington, must, by law, be wearing a cowbell. Hens are prohibited from laying eggs before 8 A.M. and after 4 P.M. in Norfolk, Virginia.

There was once a serious rooster problem in Kenilworth, Illinois. The populace became fed up with being suddenly and rudely awakened by these crowing birds. So the village passed a unique piece of legislation that states that a rooster may crow whenever he desires, but in order to exercise this right, he must first place himself three hundred feet from any house inhabited by human beings.

Have a few mules on your farm? Don't ever walk

behind one of them while plowing a field if you don't at the same time hold a conversation with the beast. In Kentucky you could be fined for "negligence." And it's against the law to lose your temper and viciously kick a mule anywhere in Arizona, while in Maine you are not allowed to "set a mule on fire."

Even farmers who file for divorce are carefully covered by legislation in Louisiana: "The fruits hanging by the roots on the lands belonging separately to either the husband or the wife, at the time of the dissolution of the marriage, are equally divided between the husband and the wife."

In Bedford, Massachusetts, farmers are banned from taking their goats into town and then letting them graze on a sidewalk or get in the way of people on the streets. Hartford, Connecticut, outlaws the racing of harnessed goats down a city street.

Horses are not allowed to enter the city of Fountain Inn, South Carolina, unless they are attired in pants. And in Charleston, South Carolina, lawmakers went one better. They passed a loony law that requires all horses that pull carriages to wear diapers. To go without diapers on a city street brings a stiff fine and jail term.

Fort Lauderdale, Florida, has an unusual ordinance governing how horses may be seen publicly on the city's streets during evening hours. The animal must have a taillight and a horn attached!

Hogs not eating the feed you have on hand? What can and cannot be legally fed to hogs is covered by law in Taylorville, Illinois. Razor blades are strictly prohibited.

Want some company on those long and cold winter nights? *The little community of Clawson, Michigan,*

has a local law that makes it perfectly legal for a farmer to "sleep with his pigs, cows, horses, goats and chickens." But he can't have any of these animals in his home during the day or "after the sun rises in the morning."

In the state of Delaware a farmer can't graze his cattle between the curb and a building on a city street. Echo, Oregon, has a special statute that declares it legal for a citizen to "catch, kill, and cook the roaming chickens of a neighbor."

Pigs can be confiscated in Philadelphia, Pennsylvania, if they are caught roaming within fourteen miles of the Delaware River where boats are navigating. The pigs will be left alone if they are wearing yokes or rings. If the animal is found without such contraptions, what is known as a "Guardian of the Poor" can pick the pig up and give it to a family in need of meat.

Like to treat your cow to a good night's sleep but don't want to put her in a dirty old barn with the animals? You can't keep her in a tenement house anywhere in the state of Kentucky. Nor can you get away with keeping chickens in a Cumberland, Maryland, hotel room. Even Massachusetts came up with a law that outlaws "swine" from being boarded in an apartment or a house.

But a city in that state—Boston—long ago took a radically different approach. It passed a law requiring all hotels to provide clean and comfortable accommodations for their guest's horses.

Loony Barber and
Beauty Legislation

BARBERS WORKING IN Waterloo, Nebraska, are banned from eating onions between the hours of 7 A.M. and 7 P.M. A barber who does have onions for lunch can be fined and his shop temporarily closed.

An old law in Oklahoma forbids its female population to undertake doing their own hair without being licensed by the state. Violators can expect to be prosecuted. Nebraska has a similar law, which makes it illegal for a mother to give her daughter a permanent unless the mother has filed for and purchased a state license.

Schoolteachers who work in Arkansas can't consider "bobbing" their hair. The law is specific when it declares that no pay raises will be authorized for teachers who violate this code.

If you have plans to go out for the evening, you'd better get your hair cut sometime during the day in Buffalo, New York. It's against the law for a barber to cut hair after 6:30 P.M.

A woman isn't allowed to cut her own hair without her husband's permission if she happens to live in

Michigan. In accordance with this law, a woman's hair doesn't even belong to her; it is rightfully owned by the man of the house. *And Wisconsin has a law that simply stops anyone—even the woman herself—from cutting a woman's hair.*

If you need a haircut or a nice comfortable shave, Omaha, Nebraska, is a good place to go. Just don't ask the barber also to shave your chest! A city ordinance bans barbers from shaving a customer's hairy chest. Barbers who do provide this service can have their license revoked!

It may be hot in that southern California barbershop if there isn't any air-conditioning. Yet you are out of luck if you get thirsty and would like a nice cold cola. It's illegal to sell soft drinks in barbershops located anywhere in the Golden State. Having soft-drink machines on the premises is included in this restriction.

Women are required by law to shave if they live in or around Carrizozo, New Mexico. It's strictly forbidden for a female to appear unshaven in public. The law applies to a woman's legs as well as face. Presumably the male population of Carrizozo can go as bearded and fuzzy as they please.

If you're looking for a bargain haircut and want to shop around, Georgia isn't the place to do this. Barbers there aren't allowed to advertise their prices in any manner.

The great Orange Juice State is extremely rough on women who spend a lot of time at a beauty salon. Females are prohibited by Florida law from falling asleep while sitting under a hair dryer. The customer can be fined, as can the person who owns the salon.

Erie, Pennsylvania, has a similar ordinance on the books but its law applies only to men. A man is not allowed to go to sleep while sitting in a barber's chair and getting a shave.

And in Binghamton, New York, a barber can lose his license if he allows a customer to fall asleep in one of his barber chairs, even during slack periods. But that law also holds the customer responsible.

Illinois covers the entire barbershop in its legislation. No one, not even a friend just in for a chat, is allowed to sleep anywhere in a barbershop. And in Hawaii neither the barber nor the customer may grab a catnap in the shop.

Morrisville, Pennsylvania, women are required by law to buy a special permit if they wish to wear any kind of cosmetics, including rouge, lipstick, and eye shadow. In this same community men aren't allowed to be shaved by someone else or even to shave themselves without a special permit.

Don't expect to have your feet powdered in a Louisiana beautician's establishment. And don't ask for a cold-cream foot rub either! A state law forbids beauty operators to perform these services on a customer's feet.

Connecticut has several unique state laws regulating various areas of the barbering business. One old law requires a haircut to be round and "to fit a cap." Another says that men are banned from getting a shave or shaving themselves on Sunday. Lastly, no one—a barber or other private citizen—can throw away used razor blades. (What do they do with them?) Memphis, Tennessee, doesn't have this sort of problem because in this city it's against the law to sell anyone a razor. Blades aren't mentioned.

Tennessee has an old law that doesn't let a barber use a brush on a customer's hair. But Hawaii's barbers have to be careful about how they brush the loose hair from a customer's shoulders. The Hawaiian law prohibits doing this with a "neck duster," whatever that may be.

Massachusetts has a variety of special statutes: citizens of that state can't shave while driving an automobile on a public street or highway. A man is prohibited from going into a beauty shop to have his hair dyed or to get a permanent wave.

The middle of Main Street is not the place to shave in Tylertown, Mississippi, which has passed a law outlawing such a dastardly deed. And shaving during any daylight hours is against the law in Poplar Bluff, Missouri.

Children should love going to a barbershop in Elkhart, Indiana. The barber is prohibited from scaring a child into being quiet by threatening to cut off his or her ears.

If there are any husbands in Glastonburg, Connecticut, who still use razor strops, they aren't allowed to use them to whip their wives. In Milwaukee, Wisconsin, barbers can't use powder puffs while cutting a customer's hair. And Hawaii doesn't let their barbers use a shaving brush even to lather a customer's chin.

There are mustache laws in a number of areas in the nation. Here is one: Binghamton, New York, won't let ninth-grade students grow a mustache, nor will anyone with a mustache—including a teacher—be allowed in a classroom.

Forget to shave on Saturday night in preparation for attending church on Sunday morning? You'll just have to go as you are if you live anywhere in the state of Ohio. Lawmakers there passed a law that prohibits men from shaving on the Sabbath. Any man caught shaving on Sunday can be fined!

In Illinois if you operate a barbershop and need some extra cash, you aren't allowed to rent the shop space as a bedroom after working hours.

Lawmakers in Los Angeles, California, really had to think hard to come up with this one: a shop can't have a striped barber pole on the sidewalk in front of it.

You'll find this hard to believe: long hair is banned for Harvard undergraduates in Cambridge, Massachusetts.

Finally, if you want to grow a stylish goatee, you may have some problems in Massachusetts. The state has an old ordinance that declares you aren't allowed to have a goatee unless you first pay a special license fee for the privilege of wearing one in public.

Laughable Laws that Especially Affect Kids and Teenagers

TEENAGERS ARE PROHIBITED from undertaking one good extra-money sideline in Newport News, Virginia. A law says you can't go around collecting used bottles, old paper, rags, and other types of sellable junk. The law further states that you aren't allowed to try and sell such materials if you do collect them.

You may have a child who just loves turtles and you may even want to pick up a turtle for a birthday present. Turtles are fine to have as pets in Key West, Florida, but a local law makes it clear that your child can't hold a turtle race within the limits of the beautiful city.

An ordinance in La Crosse, Wisconsin, bans checker playing in public. And in the quiet little community of Lead, South Dakota, you aren't allowed to light firecrackers on a trolley car track. Lastly, no child can have candy cigarettes in the entire state of North Dakota, where it's illegal for such cigarettes to be sold.

It's OK for kids to go fishing in Louisville, Kentucky. And it's all right for them to own bow and arrow sets. But don't put them together, because a Louisville law states that you can't shoot fish with a bow and arrow!

New York laws are just the opposite. They allow you to catch fish with a bow and arrow. But in Winchester, Massachusetts, no one is allowed to shoot a bow and arrow under any circumstances.

Never try to carry an ice-cream cone in your pocket while visiting or just passing through Lexington, Kentucky. This particular city has an ordinance that prohibits such transport.

Kids in Wichita, Kansas, can't buy or use a slingshot and they can be arrested simply for carrying one! The law in Pateros, Washington, declares that no kid can "wear a slingshot." And in Olympia, Washington, you aren't allowed to "use" a slingshot. But in quiet little Moscow, Idaho, you can own a slingshot after you have obtained the permission of the chief of police.

A special law in Richmond, Virginia, prohibits children from drawing pictures and scribbling or writing on city sidewalks. *In Hartford, Connecticut, you aren't allowed to cross a street while walking on your hands.* However, it seems that Hanford, California, community leaders like kids better, since they have passed an ordinance that makes it illegal for anyone to try and stop a child from playfully jumping over puddles of water.

Boys aren't allowed to throw snowballs at trees in the town of Mount Pulaski, Illinois (the lawmakers seem to believe girls won't even try).

In Oklahoma City, Oklahoma, a law bans the throwing of snowballs at anything. Nor can you toss snowballs within the city limits of Watertown, New York.

Wilmington, Delaware, seems to be against kids

having fun in wintertime. That city won't let them slide on an ice-covered sidewalk. Indiana has a law prohibiting kids from working on Sundays, unless they are *under* fourteen years of age! There is an even stranger law on the books in Omaha, Nebraska. A parent can be arrested if his or her child can't hold back that burp while a church service is in session.

In Spokane, Washington, a kid can't buy any flavor or size lollipop within the city's boundaries. On Sunday in South Dakota, you can't go out and buy a quart of ice cream. And Evanston, Illinois, doesn't let its children have any ice-cream sodas on the Sabbath. To get around this old law, William C. Garwood, a druggist, started serving "Sundays" in 1882. However, church leaders violently objected to his naming the confection after the Sabbath day, and the name was changed to "sundae."

Kingsport, Tennessee, has made it illegal to sell soft

drinks during the time of church services on Sunday. And Georgia still retains an old law that doesn't let kids swim on Sunday in certain specified places. The law states that you can't "bathe in a stream or a pond in view of a road to a church."

In Denver, Colorado, no kid is allowed to lift his or her feet higher than the front of his or her bicycle when riding down a city street. And in Danbury, Connecticut, you can be arrested for riding your bike faster than sixty-five miles an hour. In the city of Cleveland, Ohio, "Look, Ma, no hands" is illegal—you can be halted if caught riding a bicycle with your hands off the handlebars. But Baldwin Park, California, tops them all—they won't let you ride a bike in, or into, a swimming pool.

Kids aren't allowed to roller-skate on a city street after 8:00 P.M. in Milwaukee, Wisconsin. You can't ride a tricycle or do any roller-skating on the sidewalks in Moscow, Idaho. And it's illegal to roller-skate down a public street anywhere in Quincy, Massachusetts. Lastly, in Portland, Oregon, the law says you can never roller-skate into a public rest room.

Beebe River, New Hampshire, is a small town with a law that makes it illegal for a child to tease or torment a dog. Don't chase any squirrels in Topeka, Kansas; a statute there prohibits kids from "annoying" these furry little animals.

In Olympia, Washington, it's not illegal to sell a beanshooter or a peashooter. But a kid can't own, use, or even carry one within the city limits. The city of New York has a law that declares beanshooters may not be sold to kids. And in Arkansas, it's a misdemeanor if you are even caught with a beanshooter in your possession.

Children are prohibited from walking a tightrope within the city limits of Rochester, New York. This same city won't let kids collect cigar stubs as a hobby.

You can't do something even as harmless as juggling in Hood River, Oregon. An exception to this law is made if you request a special license.

Like to sit on a garbage can to rest after running down the block? It's against the law if the can is in Montgomery, Alabama.

Kites seem to have been the object of much interest on the part of lawmakers: you are banned from flying a kite in Norfolk, Virginia, and also in Washington, D.C. But you can fly a kite in Danbury, Connecticut, if you first get a special permit from the mayor. In Meridian, Mississippi, kids are, but businessmen are not, allowed to fly kites on the city streets.

Would you like to try rolling barrels down the street? Pensacola, Florida, isn't the best place for this activity. The city has a law banning kids from barrel rolling. And you can't roll hoops down any street in Treadelphia, West Virginia, or Watkins Glen, New York.

Springfield, Illinois, has a strange law that won't allow a kid to walk astraddle a fence without the owner's permission. And in Macon, Georgia, kids aren't allowed to climb a fence in order to get into a cemetery.

These laws will probably be popular with the average child: in Boston, Massachusetts, kids can't take a bath on a Sunday. But the best place to be during a long, cold winter is Clinton, Indiana. The law there makes it illegal to bathe at all during the winter!

A child can be arrested in Atlanta, Georgia, if he or she makes faces at other kids while they are in a school classroom during a study period. And no children are allowed to attend public schools in Raleigh County, West Virginia, if their breath smells like "wild onions." Parents are prohibited from insulting a teacher in front of pupils throughout Arkansas. Nor can students insult one another.

Staten Island, New York, has an unusual ordinance controlling what a father may call his son. No father, no matter how upset, can legally say the words "faggot" or "queer" to his male offspring in an effort to cure the boy's "girlie behavior." A parent can be charged with "child abuse," and will be prosecuted.

No skunk hunting by kids in Pennsylvania? That's right! That state passed a special law entitled Act for the Better Protection of Skunks. In Minnesota it's "unlawful to tease or torment skunks or polecats." And in Alabama you could be arrested for simply calling a friend a skunk.

A kid can't do cartwheels or any other acrobatics on a sidewalk in Denver, Colorado. The reason? Because such activities might scare horses!

Let's look at a few more of the most unusual laws pertaining to kids and teenagers: you can be kicked out of a movie theater in Winnetka, Illinois, if you take your shoes off and your feet stink. In Yuma, Arizona, you'll be forced to take a dose of castor oil if you get caught stealing citrus fruit from an orchard. You aren't allowed to eat watermelon in the Magnolia Street cemetery if you live in Spartanburg, South Carolina. And you can't drink milk on a train passing through North Carolina.

Loony Gun, Hunting, and Fishing Legislation

In California you can be convicted of a misdemeanor if you are caught shooting at any kind of game *except a whale* from a moving automobile or an airplane.

In Norfolk County, Virginia, hunters don't stand a chance if they shoot animals while both feet are firmly planted on the ground. By law, you can hunt birds and game with a rifle only from at least fifteen feet above the ground!

Truro, Mississippi, blends hunting skills with a young man's marriage plans. A young lover, before being allowed to marry the girl of his dreams, must first "prove himself manly" enough for the task. How does a suitor accomplish such a feat? Quite simple! He merely goes out into the woods and bags six blackbirds—or three crows. The dead birds must then be presented to his prospective father-in-law as proof of the young man's masculinity.

Two of our states are doing their bit to save the endangered whale. Legislators in Ohio passed a statute that specifically outlaws whale fishing in any of the

state's lakes, streams, or rivers on Sundays. *And Oklahoma has gone further, by banning fishing for whales seven days a week in the state's inland waters!*

In Louisiana it is illegal to rob a bank and then shoot at a bank teller with a water pistol.

You may enjoy duck hunting and you might even like to take a mule along for the day. Don't try this in the state of Kansas. It's against Kansas law to "hunt ducks with a mule." Violators can be fined and jailed for such a dastardly act. But an old federal statute singles out postmasters with a more severe restriction: a postmaster is not allowed to go duck hunting anywhere in the entire United States.

It's strictly illegal to fish while on horseback in Washington, D.C., and in Colorado. Pennsylvania lawmakers are even tougher. They prohibit a sportsman from even taking a horse along on a fishing trip, whether or not he's riding the animal.

Michigan may be considered an absolute paradise for

those who enjoy duck hunting. State law imposes a minimum twenty-five-dollar fine on anyone scaring wild ducks during the official hunting season.

A woman in the state of Ohio is legally allowed to destroy her mate's hunting and fishing "junk" whenever she pleases. She can even burn his old clothing as well.

Santa Clara, California, has outlawed the drugging of trout in inland lakes or rivers in order to catch the fish. Taking the opposite tack, Toltec, Colorado, refuses to allow fishermen to catch their limit with their bare hands; the law insists that they use a fishing pole with hook and bait attached.

Don't even think of going to Berea, Kentucky, and trying to shoot clay pigeons "during the breeding season." That's a strange law! It doesn't bother clarifying whether it means the breeding season for clay pigeons or for other, more hot-blooded birds.

Tennessee has an old law that prohibits the use of a lasso to catch a fish. Nor can you fish with a lasso in the state of Washington. Washington also prevents fishermen from using a gun to shoot their quarry! The same holds true in little Hazlehurst, Mississippi.

Colorado follows California in prohibiting hunting from an airplane. More specifically, the law says that no one is allowed to duck hunt from an airplane in flight! Apparently our forebears from coast to coast indulged in a sport we've heard little about. For example, Los Angeles, California, retains an old ordinance that makes it illegal for a person to "shoot a hare or a jackrabbit from any car of a trolley in transit on the city streets."

New York City has a similar quaint piece of legisla-

tion that specifically bans the shooting of rabbits while standing or sitting in the rear of a trolley car. Denver, Colorado, outlaws the shooting of jackrabbits from the back *window* of a streetcar rolling along a city street. And in Idaho the lawmakers pulled out all stops in a concentrated effort to stop those madmen with guns from riding the rails. Idaho law states that no kind of hunting can be undertaken while riding on the "interurban trolley system," and further, that no one is allowed to "shoot game birds or wild animals" within fifty feet of trolley tracks.

Oklahoma law declares that the only time a person may legally carry a gun is when he or she is being "chased by an Indian."

The Bluegrass State is well known for a few of its stranger pieces of loony legislation. Kentucky legislators actually passed a law making it a criminal offense to fire a gun that wasn't loaded!

In Spades, Indiana, you aren't allowed to open a can of food by shooting at it with a revolver! The law says nothing about shooting open a can of food with a rifle or a machine gun.

In Port Allen, Louisiana, hunting rabbits within the city limits is prohibited; in New York City you may not hunt birds or rabbits in a cemetery; in Sapulpa, Oklahoma, you can't shoot game in a city park. In Buffalo, however, a law banning the use of weapons in city parks and playgrounds specifies only bows and arrows.

You might try your hand at hunting camels and buffalo, but this might be a problem in Arizona and Wyoming. Fort Warren, Wyoming, is tough on buffalo-shooting buffs. It's against the law to stand inside the barracks and fire at a buffalo from one of the windows. And Kingman, Arizona, prohibits all camel hunting within the limits of the city.

Here's a warning for parents of small children in Georgia. You can be "armed to the teeth," even in metropolitan Atlanta, if you simply follow the letter of the old law that says every weapon "must be in full view" at all times. But take note: "weapons" in this case include toy cap guns and water pistols as well as toy rubber knives.

Georgia has another old piece of legislation, which is designed to stop people from firing a gun at a picnic. And if you are hunting in Michigan and have lots of luck you'd better plan on taking home all of the game you bag. It's illegal to leave any dead animals on a road or highway in the state. And in Cleveland, Ohio, you can't even catch a mouse unless you have a valid hunting license.

Be careful about avenging insults if you live in Massachusetts. An old piece of legislation outlaws any form of dueling when it is undertaken between two opponents who wish to use water pistols. Yes, the law specifies *water pistols*. And in North Andover, Massachusetts, a local law prohibits citizens from carrying what are loosely defined as "space guns."

Beware, too, if you plan on duck hunting at night in Essex Falls, New Jersey. You might alarm your prey, and the law there states that ducks are not allowed to be heard quacking after 10:00 P.M.

Laughable Laws
Concerning Food and
Drink

THE *ENCYCLOPAEDIA BRITANNICA* is actually outlawed in the state of Texas, for a statute prohibits Texans from purchasing, stores from selling, and others from owning a set of these enlightening books. Why? The *Britannica* contains a formula in one of its volumes for manufacturing home brew.

You will really get good service in restaurants when you stop to eat anywhere in Pennsylvania. The law requires that all eating establishments be equipped with wheelchairs and a stretcher before food can be served to customers.

Do you like to nibble on pretzels while sipping a glass of beer? Forget this if you stop in for a drink after work at a North Dakota bar. It's against the law to serve pretzels and beer at the same time in any bar, club, or eating establishment.

Delaware prohibits everyone from flying over a large body of water unless they are carrying plenty of good food and drink in the airplane. The kind of drink isn't specified.

No waiter or waitress in Topeka, Kansas, is allowed to serve a customer wine in a teacup under any circumstances, while in Nebraska the state legislature has stipulated that in any establishment that sells or serves beer or wine, a large pot of hot soup must be seen cooking on the premises.

Kentucky women have been given the legal right to put castor oil in their hubby's alcoholic drinks to stop him from drinking. It's not only a wife's right to spike his drinks, the state considers it to be one of her moral duties.

Duluth, Minnesota, has a law that makes it illegal to let a dog, horse, or any other animal sleep in a bakery. (The law also bans dogs from napping in a barbershop or a beauty salon.) Nor can any animal sleep in a cheese factory in Indiana or in a restaurant in Kentucky.

And in Springs, Pennsylvania, the law specifies that a married man cannot purchase any form of booze without having the consent of his loving wife—in writing!

Got a hangover? The night before leave a bad taste in your mouth? Don't try gargling in public anywhere in the state of Louisiana. You just have to live with that cotton-in-the-mouth feeling. Nor can a person gargle publicly in Hot Springs, Arkansas.

In Birmingham, Alabama, it's against the law for a bartender or a restaurant owner or manager to take up a broom. They simply aren't allowed to sweep the floors in their own place of business.

Buckland, Alaska, has outlawed any kind of intoxicating drinks. The town's very direct law declares: "No

one shall carry or bring intoxicating liquors to this village. If anyone brings or carries intoxicating liquor, he is to be sent out from this town.''

Nyala, Nevada, passed an ordinance regarding a man's (but not a woman's) buying his buddies a drink while out on the town: no man is ever allowed to treat more than three drinkers besides himself at any one period in a day.

Don't try to be friendly and share your booze with another person by passing the bottle around in Cleveland, Ohio. It's against the law there for more than one individual to sip from the same bottle of whiskey. And it's also unlawful for two or more people to get drunk together if they all take turns drinking from the same whiskey bottle, so they get you on *two* counts if you get drunk sharing the bottle.

In LeFors, Texas, it's illegal to take more than three swallows of beer at any one time while standing on your feet! So sit in a chair before you chug-a-lug.

Colorado Springs, Colorado, has banned hostesses and waiters or waitresses from insulting customers in a lounge, bar, or eating establishment. To toss invectives at a patron can bring a stiff fine.

Natchez, Mississippi, has a strange ordinance making it illegal for an elephant to guzzle beer. The law says nothing about the person who offers the beast the brew.

A New Jersey law makes it illegal for people to slurp their soup. Anyone who is apprehended slurping soup in a public restaurant is subject to arrest, a fine, and a possible term in jail.

And would you believe that in Fairbanks, Alaska, it's against the law to feed any kind of alcoholic beverages—beer, wine, or the stronger stuff—to a moose?

Stay out of saloons if you are on horseback in Ellensburg, Washington. That community prohibits you from riding your horse into a saloon or tavern. Prescott, Arizona, and the entire state of California have also banned citizens from going into a saloon while astride a horse. This ban does not govern in Burns, Oregon, where you can commit this act by paying an admission fee.

Michigan legislators once passed a strict law that applies to their justices of the peace. Court proceedings cannot be held in a bar or tavern.

In St. Louis, Missouri, it is illegal to sit on the curb of any city street and drink beer from a bucket.

Corvallis, Oregon, isn't the best place in the nation

to try and sober up if you are a woman. There's a law that forbids ''young ladies'' to drink coffee after the hour of 6:00 P.M.

And in Hawaii it's not lawful to whistle while in a bar or nightclub.

A true friend to the thirsty people of the world is the small city of Casper, Wyoming. No one is allowed to loan city water to a neighbor—unless the water is for drinking.

Mourners attending a wake in Boston, Massachusetts, aren't allowed to have more than three sandwiches at one time, no matter how hungry they may think they are.

In Gary, Indiana, the local citizenry are prohibited from attending a movie house or other theater and from

riding in a public streetcar within at least four hours after eating garlic. And of all things, you can't throw onions at anyone in Princeton, Texas.

The whole state of Texas bans calendars showing scantily dressed or nude women in taverns and nightclubs. So you'll never find a *Playboy* calendar on the wall of your favorite drinking establishment!

And also in Texas, it took a law to determine that rum-flavored ice cream is legally classified as ice cream and is not in the same category as an alcoholic beverage.

Hostesses, bartenders, waiters, and waitresses in any Arkansas drinking establishment are prohibited from taking tips, directly or indirectly, from one of the customers. The same kind of law is also in effect in Key West, Florida.

North Dakota prohibits employees from falling asleep

in the restaurant or dining room of a hotel, while its neighbor South Dakota prohibits its citizens from going into a cheese factory, lying down, and falling asleep. This same kind of legislation is also on the books in Houston, Texas.

And last but by far not the least, Kentucky has a law that says that anyone who has been drinking "is sober" until he or she "cannot hold onto the ground."

Loony Police and Fire Fighter Legislation

An 1899 Tennessee law requires keepers of hotels and lodging houses over two stories high to provide a rope to serve as a fire escape in every lodging room above the second story that has an outside window. The rope has to be at least one inch in diameter and securely fastened within the room as near to a window as practicable. It has to be long enough to reach through the window to the ground outside and to be of strong material and as fireproof as possible.

Police officers working in East Peoria, Illinois, must be willing to wear an American-flag patch on their uniform. To refuse to comply can result in suspension from duty.

It's illegal in Montgomery, Alabama, for a person to refuse the orders of a fire fighter when he or she tells the person to leave a burning house. No reason for not leaving will be considered.

It's against the law in Kentucky for a minister to be arrested while he or she is preaching in a public worship service. Any police officer who does arrest a working member of the clergy is fined not less than ten dollars and not more than fifty dollars.

Women should be up in arms over this strange law in St. Louis, Missouri. No female wearing a nightgown, sheer or otherwise, can be rescued by an on-duty fire fighter. The law is specific when it states that a woman of any age must always be fully dressed before a fire fighter can help her during a fire. This seems to be a burning question in St. Louis!

Texas recently passed what is known as its anticrime law. This statute actually requires a criminal to give his or her intended victim twenty-four hours' notice, either orally or in writing. The victim must clearly be told the nature of the crime to be committed! And he or she must also be given the time and place at which it will happen.

If you are a fire fighter in Washington, D.C., you should be cautious about what you do while waiting for fires. Playing cards in a firehouse is forbidden, as are all forms of gambling activities. You can't legally play even solitaire or a nongambling card game with your coworkers.

Within thirty minutes of your arrival in Albuquerque, New Mexico, you are required by an old law to "check all shooting irons" at the local police station.

According to a little-known law on the books in Missouri, state police officers are prohibited from chewing tobacco while performing their duties. And in Rocky Mount, North Carolina, on-duty police officers aren't allowed to dip snuff. Dipping snuff can bring a fine and probation for the cop.

Anyone wishing to be a fire fighter should certainly

consider relocating to Marblehead, Massachusetts. The city fathers have decreed that any fire company that answers an alarm and goes forth to fight a fire must, by law, be given three full gallons of rum by the grateful citizenry.

Omaha, Nebraska, has an odd statute that says it's against the law for a cop to walk around with his hands in his pockets. Such activity can result in strong disciplinary action and even in dismissal from the force.

Pity the poor cop who walks a beat in this same city while the rain pours down. According to another local statute, he or she must never be seen carrying an umbrella.

Let's hope you don't have a fire in your home or business if you are located in New Britain, Connecticut. *The speed limit for fire trucks is a mere twenty-five miles per hour. Fire trucks are prohibited from going any faster even when going to a fire.*

It could be an even more trying wait for help in New

Orleans, Louisiana. In that city, fire engines must always stop for red traffic lights.

There are compensations for being a law officer. A little community called Homer, Illinois, has a city ordinance that declares that only a uniformed police officer can legally carry a slingshot. And in tiny Harriman, Tennessee, the law designates the sheriff as the "official cider taster" for all the cider sold within the city.

According to how fast he or she can perform his or her duties, a fire fighter in Ziegler, Illinois, could either get rich or starve. The only fire fighters who get paid for their services are the four men who first arrive at the scene of a fire. All the others receive nothing more than a thank-you and a pat on the back.

No one has to worry over whether police officers will talk about him or her behind his or her back in Key West, Florida. The city has banned on-duty policemen from gossiping. And it's even nicer in Halsey, Nebraska. There the town constable can never be rude to the general public. Per the statute, he "must remember his manners."

Fire hydrants are sacred objects in some cities. For example, in Helena, Montana, no one may tie a horse to a fireplug within the city limits; in Detroit, Michigan, a crocodile can't be tied to a hydrant; and in the nation's capital, a law prohibits bringing mules into town and "hitching" them to a fire-alarm box.

Keep right on smiling when a New Jersey law enforcement officer is talking to you—even if he's also writing you out a ticket. It's against the law in New Jersey to "frown" at a police officer.

The cop's image is carefully protected in South Dakota. No movie can be shown in the state if the film contains any scenes of a police officer being struck, beaten, or offensively treated in any manner.

Fire fighters are not allowed to make or sell hooked rugs while on duty in Springfield, Massachusetts. And in Racine, Wisconsin, it's against the law for a citizen to wake up a fire fighter who is sleeping, no matter what the problem may be.

An old Tennessee law requires the maintenance of the state arsenal in the north end of the basement of the state capitol.

If a sheriff was part of a lynch mob in Ohio, the county in which the lynching took place is liable to the victim for a sum of up to five hundred dollars. And in St. Joseph, Missouri, fire fighters who are lounging at the fire hall are not allowed to run around in their undershirt. And finally, Maine has a great law on the books when it comes to cops making an arrest. *No police officer is allowed to arrest a dead man!*

Laughable Laws
Concerning Automobiles
and Driving

Mᴀssᴀᴄʜᴜsᴇᴛᴛs ʟᴇᴀᴅs ᴛʜᴇ way with an example of outdated legalistic verbiage. You can try and figure out exactly what it means: "Whoever operates an automobile or motorcycle on any public way—laid out under authority of law recklessly or while under the influence of liquor shall be punished; thereby imposing upon the motorist the duty of finding out at his peril whether certain highways had been laid out recklessly or while under the influence of liquor before driving his car over them."

Detroit, Michigan, has banned couples from making love in an automobile unless the act takes place while the vehicle is parked on the couple's own property.

Springfield, Massachusetts, has a similar ordinance, except its law applies specifically to taxi drivers. Cabbies are prohibited from making love in the front seat of their vehicle during their working shift. (Guess it's okay to do it in the backseat, as the law doesn't mention this location.)

Don't plan on going to a drive-in movie, or even to the grocery store, if you take your wife out in quiet Corning, Iowa. That town has a law that makes it illegal for a man to ask his wife to get into the car and ride with him. And Spencer, Iowa, another small town, declares that a man cannot ever ask any female, whatever her age or marital status, to get into his car and go for a ride. The man will be charged with "solicitation."

Driving through Norman, Oklahoma? Put down that comic book. The law says you can't read comics while driving an automobile.

Brewton, Alabama, has taken stern measures to prevent shipwrecks. Legislators there say you can't "drive a motorboat" on a city street. Nor can you fish from a motorboat while it is being driven down a highway or street.

The law in Green Bay, Wisconsin, outlaws cars that drip on the pavement. The fine? One dollar for each dripped drop found under the car.

State legislators have passed a bill that prohibits "uncaged bears" from riding in an automobile, or even from being carried in the trunk, while the car is on a Missouri highway.

In Detroit, Michigan, Automobile City, it's illegal for a driver to "ogle" a woman from a moving automobile. Also in Detroit, you are banned from using any kind of pennant to decorate your car in order to be noticed or to impress your girlfriend.

Tacoma, Washington, has an unusual old ordinance designed to lessen crime within the city limits. The law, in all seriousness states: "It is mandatory for a motorist

with criminal intentions to stop at the city limits and telephone the chief of police as he is entering the town.''

Dogs are strictly forbidden to ride in ambulances in Westport, Massachusetts. They can't be taken along even if their master or mistress is being taken to the hospital. But you could be in deep trouble obeying this law in Springfield, Illinois. The law there says a person can't abandon a dog for any reason.

Utah declares by law that birds in the state always have the right of way on all highways. Springfield, Ohio, bans motorists from cleaning and dusting their vehicle's interior while the automobile is being driven down a city street. Cows in Farmington, Connecticut, have as much right on a highway or a road as do motorists and their vehicle.

If you leave your automobile on a street in Milwaukee, Wisconsin, for over two hours at one time, the car must be securely hitched to a horse! That's the law in the beer capital of the world.

Hammond, Indiana, has what is known as its Castor Oil Ordinance. If any driver is picked up for littering the streets, the automatic penalty is "one good dose of castor oil," to be administered by the police department.

New Mexico outlaws vehicle horns and whistles if the horn or whistle has what is considered to be "an inharmonious sound."

A law in Pleasantville, Iowa, makes it mandatory for cars and trucks on the road at night to be preceded by a man carrying a bright red lantern. No vehicle is allowed to come into or be driven through Pleasantville without this lantern.

Civic leaders in California's El Dorado County knew how to stop reckless drivers. Their 1907 law declares: "Speed upon county roads will be limited to ten miles an hour unless the motorist sees a bailiff who does not appear to have had a drink in thirty days, then the driver will be permitted to make what he can."

A similar law can be found in Jackson, Tennessee. There a "herald" must walk or run in front of every automobile as it is being driven through the town.

It could be rather difficult for bicycle riders in Osceola, Missouri. Whenever a person on a bicycle approaches a horse-drawn carriage on the street, he or she must stop and then ask permission of the carriage driver to pass. The law also says the request must be "courteous."

When you drive up to the city limits of Suffolk, Virginia, you may have to walk through town. A local ordinance doesn't allow an automobile or other motorized vehicle to be driven under its own power in the town. (Maybe you could push it?)

And in Silverton, Texas, you aren't allowed to drive within three miles of the city limits.

Even elephants are covered by special ordinances in Orlando, Florida. If an elephant is left tied to a parking meter, the parking fee has to be paid exactly as it would be for a motor vehicle.

City fathers in Memphis, Tennessee, came up with an excellent driving law. They made it clear that no one is to be allowed to drive a car in their city while the driver is sound asleep. What foresight! And in Birmingham, Alabama, it's illegal for a driver to be blindfolded while operating an automobile in the city.

Nevada prohibits anyone from driving a camel on a public highway.

A number of odd laws simply cover activities that may or may not transpire on highways and public roads. In Maine no one is allowed to carry a "naked scythe sharpened" while on a public thoroughfare. This is punishable by a two-dollar fine.

Tramps or bums are prohibited from building a fire on a highway in New Hampshire unless they first get permission. In both Ola, South Dakota, and Anniston, Oklahoma, no one is allowed to lie down and take a

nap in the middle of a road. And would you believe that chickens in Quitman, Georgia, are not allowed to walk across a road within the city limits? Let's hope that Quitman chickens are educated enough to know!

In Omaha, Nebraska, the law states that a man has to buy his wife new clothing every time she appears in court or with him in his place, in defense of a traffic violation. The amount to be spent on her attire must match the fine imposed on her husband by the judge.

Cabdrivers and taxis are governed by a number of unusual laws all over the nation. In Youngstown, Ohio, customers are prohibited from riding on the roof of a moving taxi. In both Colorado and Ohio, cabdrivers aren't allowed to smoke while driving a passenger around town. *Albuquerque, New Mexico, won't let its cabbies reach out and pull prospective customers into their vehicle.* All cabs in Washington, D.C., must be equipped with both a broom and a shovel. And in Birmingham, Alabama, cabbies are not allowed to sleep in their taxi while it is parked in a public place.

Loony Medical and
Dental Legislation

IF YOU WANT ice cream after dinner in Newark, New
Jersey, stock your freezer early. Ice cream is unavailable
in Newark after 6:00 P.M. unless the customer has a
doctor's written permission to buy it.

A Yukon, Oklahoma, city ordinance specifically prohibits a patient from pulling a dentist's tooth. In Georgia, a dentist is breaking the law if he is found to be
cruel to a patient. A first offense is a misdemeanor and
the penalty is a small fine. Continued acts of cruelty
will result in a suspension of the dentist's license.

Research laboratories in New York City could be in
serious trouble with the law. *It's illegal in New York
for anyone to carry bones or a skeleton into a building
without first having written permission.*

No dentist in Jamestown, New York, is allowed to
use hypnotism on a patient. Violators can be fined up
to $250 and jailed for up to thirty days. Hypnotism in
this community is looked upon as a form of "sorcery"
and is "the work of the Devil."

In Moscow, Idaho, neither doctors *nor* dentists are

allowed to use hypnotism in their practice of the medical arts.

Virginia has a strange old law establishing when their citizens may or may not bathe. It's illegal to take a bath unless you first have your doctor's permission. And Boston, Massachusetts, has an ordinance prohibiting the taking of a bath unless you are *ordered* to do so by a physician.

Have to spend some time in the hospital and don't want to leave your pets home? Let's hope it's not in Wadsworth, Kansas. Cats and other household pets are forbidden to accompany patients into the Veterans Administration hospital.

Port Huron, Michigan, has a statute that prohibits ambulances from going over the limit of twenty miles per hour, for whatever the emergency. And in Chestertown, Maryland, if you are in an accident and picked up by an ambulance belonging to the city, the ambulance will be charged to you at the rate of twenty-five cents for each mile you are carried.

If you like to have a good chew of tobacco now and then, be careful when in Connecticut. One old state law prohibits anyone from chewing tobacco without the written permission of a licensed physician. To chew tobacco without a prescription will bring a fine and some time in the local jailhouse.

Troutcreek, Utah, has a law that every outdoors type has always wanted to know about but is afraid to ask. The funny law? A pharmacist isn't able to sell gunpowder to a customer for use as a headache remedy!

Be extremely careful if you have a successful dental practice in South Foster, Rhode Island. A local law in this community, passed many long years ago, says a dentist who by accident pulls a patient's wrong tooth must willingly have his own identical tooth pulled—by the village blacksmith.

Any kid who has the whooping cough can't be seen on the streets without carrying a large warning sign around his or her neck. That's how it is in Bloomfield, New Jersey.

In Asheville, North Carolina, it's against the law to sneeze on any of the city streets. Why such a law? To protect the health of others? No! Simply because sneezing in public might frighten a horse.

Dentists with a practice in Michigan are officially classed as "mechanics." An old law in Somerville, Tennessee, declares that all dentists and dental technicians are also "mechanics." Nevertheless, dentists in North Branch, Minnesota, have it a little better than

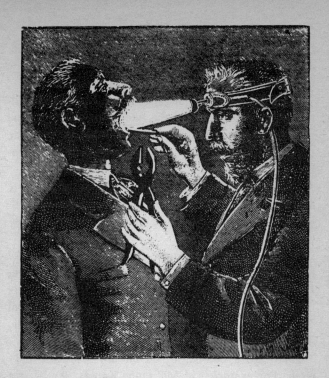

those in Michigan and Somerville for they are legally classed as "teeth and gum mechanics."

How could a man or woman practice dentistry in the state of Texas? An old law makes you wonder. *It prohibits anyone from having any kind of pliers in his or her possession.*

Houston, Mississippi, has a strange old medical law pertaining to train travel. No one is allowed to get on or get off a train in Houston without first showing a special health certificate.

Arkansas has an unusual law governing certain types of practices that aren't allowed in the state. Neither "craniology" nor "phrenology" (both occult areas dealing with the shape of the human head) can be undertaken as a profession in the realm of legitimate medicine.

You can go to every variety store in town, to five-and-tens, grocery stores, and the like, yet you should find no mothballs for sale in California. According to a state law, only licensed pharmacists are allowed to sell mothballs.

And on the Sabbath you can buy a tube of toothpaste at a drugstore in Providence, Rhode Island, but it's illegal for the same drugstore to also sell you a toothbrush.

Even if you have a favorite politician and would like to help that person get elected, you can't do it in Pekin, Illinois, if you're a doctor. An ordinance specifically bans all physicians from becoming involved in political campaigns. Nor can a doctor legally run for a public office.

There are a number of quaint laws covering false teeth. For example, in McLouth, Kansas, it's against the law to use a public drinking fountain for the purpose of washing false teeth. In Binghamton, New York, it's illegal for anyone to take a bankrupt woman's false teeth and auction them off for money to pay off some of her debts. A woman cannot wear false teeth in Vermont unless she first has her husband's written permission. Once hubby does approve, he is then held forever liable for those false teeth.

The type of teeth you have in New Orleans, Louisiana, can determine the charges against you in a fight where you bite another person. *Biting someone with your natural teeth brings a "simple assault" charge.*

But it's "aggravated assault" should you bite someone with your false teeth.

In Houston, Texas, all dogcatchers must undergo some unusual medical treatment before they can be legally qualified to hold the position. They are required to report to a psychoanalyst and be psychoanalyzed. Only after this will they be seriously considered for the job.

In Ohio no one may be classified as a "horse doctor," not even veterinarians who may actually be specializing in the medical care of horses.

Laughable Laws Concerning Guys on the Make

Be extremely careful if you're single and out drinking in the little town of Baker, Oklahoma. Leave the girl down at the other end of the bar alone if she doesn't respond to your witty conversation. Baker has passed a law that says a man can't talk to any female against her will. You could get arrested and fined for so doing.

Abilene, Texas, still retains a strict old ordinance on flirting. A woman doesn't really stand a chance to meet anyone in this city. The law actually reads: "No male person shall make remarks to or concerning, or cough or whistle at, or do anything to attract the attention of any woman upon traveling along any of the sidewalks."

It's against the law in Norfolk, Virginia, for a man to pat a female on the behind. Such activity might cost the offending male a $150 fine and sixty days in jail.

Alva C. Long, an attorney in Auburn, Washington, offers this legislative gem from his state. Seems it's illegal to get married and go on a honeymoon in the Evergreen State! Here it is: "Every person who shall

seduce and have sexual intercourse with any female of previously chaste character shall be punished by imprisonment in the state penitentiary for not more than five (5) years or in the county jail for not more than one (1) year or by a fine of $1000 or by both fine and imprisonment.''

Men wearing a mustache in Eureka, Nevada, had better be careful when out on a date or running for public office! Eureka has a law declaring: ''A mustache is a known carrier of germs and a man cannot wear one if he habitually kisses human beings.'' So much for romance and politics in Eureka!

Meet an attractive woman and courting her with little attentions? Don't offer her a cigarette if you happen to be anywhere in Illinois. That state has a law that says a man can't give away a cigarette under any circumstances.

If you are visiting Dyersburg, Tennessee, and would like to get together with an old flame, you'll have to make the contact. *She can't call you.* This town prohibits women from using the telephone to call a man and ask him for a date! A certain North Carolina town has banned massage parlors by law. Not so unusual? Maybe not, but a bit incongruous in this all-American community named *Hornytown*!

A law in Buckland, Alaska, reads: "Any persons 'getting together' must have intentions to marry and should a child result of this union the parties must marry."

Logan County, Colorado, has passed a law that forbids a man to kiss a woman "while she is asleep, without first waking her."

North Carolina retains an unusual law regarding couples who rent a hotel room for only one night. This loony legislation regulates the placement of beds in any establishment within the boundaries of the state. All must be twin beds. But each is required to be a minimum of two feet apart. Renters of a room cannot move the beds any closer. And the law also makes it a crime to make love on the floor between the beds! Does this same piece of legalese apply to motels as well?

North Carolina has another wonderful piece of loony legalese on the books. Both guys and gals are punished with a fine of $500 and as much as a six-month prison term. The law covers those who "lewdly and lasciviously associate, bed, and cohabit together, in a public or nonpublic place.''

In Macon, Georgia, they'll throw a man in jail for merely putting his arm around a girl. The old law here says that ''no man can place his arm around a woman without having a good and legal reason.''

And in Chicago, Illinois, an old piece of legislation declares that a man cannot hug a female neighbor against her wishes.

It's against the law for a man or a woman to respond to a wink or a wave given by an admiring member of the opposite sex in San Antonio, Texas. The law prohibits all flirting by using either the eyes or the hands.

Trains are not the place to make out anywhere in Wisconsin. The law there says a man can't steal a kiss from a female passenger on a train!

Tulsa, Oklahoma, actually has an ordinance against kisses that last for more than three full minutes. The law applies to both marrieds and singles alike. The lovers are required by law to pause for breath between each tender kiss. The state of Iowa is a little more lenient. It allows kisses to last for as much as, but no more than, five minutes. But in Cedar Rapids, Iowa, no one is allowed to lay a smooch on a stranger.

The law in Indianapolis, Indiana, prohibits males with hair growing over their upper lip from planting a buss on a female, whatever the circumstances. Isn't it strange? You can make love to a woman in Indianapolis, but you aren't allowed to kiss her if you sport a mustache!

Musical males are out of luck in Kalamazoo, Michigan. That city has an ordinance that prohibits a man from serenading his girlfriend, or even his wife.

And in Boston, Massachusetts, a man must have a special license to be able to serenade his girl late at night or simply to stand under her bedroom window and to sing to her.

Lastly, another unique piece of legislation out of high-minded Buckland, Alaska, where a city ordinance says: ''Any person shall not tempt any man's wife. A stranger should not stop overnight when the woman is alone.''

A Potpourri of Other
Loony Legislation

INDIANS COULD NOT testify against white persons, according to an early California law. Neither could the Chinese—because, California courts ruled, they were Indians. If the Chinese were Indians, then, according to the law, Indians were Chinese. And since the Chinese were Mongols, that made Mongols of the Indians, too. So a third law, barring marriage between white persons and Mongols, applied to Indians as well. Therefore, marriage between a white woman and her Indian spouse was declared to be illegal.

Peeping Toms are carefully covered by loony legislation within the boundaries of North Carolina. The current law could be seen as somewhat biased! Men are prohibited from peeping through a window at a woman. But a female can get away with peeping at a man under the same circumstances. And a male can't be prosecuted for peeping at another man in a state of undress!

Molesting butterflies can get you up to six months in jail and as much as a five-hundred-dollar fine if you live in the town of Pacific Grove, California.

All legislative journals and appendixes, according to an obsolete Tennessee law, must be bound in leather. No other binding will be considered as sufficient, even if cheaper.

You are allowed to hunt grizzly bears in Alaska, but the law says no one can "disturb a grizzly bear in order to take its picture."

In Arizona there is a law that says no person is allowed to hunt bullfrogs; the season is permanently closed. *And in Memphis, Tennessee, frogs are not allowed to croak after 11:00 P.M.*

Chicago, Illinois, is the only known city to have an

Ugly Law. It reads: "No person who is diseased, maimed, mutilated or in any way deformed so as to be an unsightly or disgusting object, or an improper person to be allowed in or on the public ways of other public places in this city, shall therein or thereon expose himself to public view, under a penalty of not less than one dollar nor more then $50 for each offense."

Courting that special girl and her father disapproves? There is really nothing to fear if you are after her in Wichita, Kansas. A girl's father isn't allowed to scare off his daughter's beau by taking up a gun and going after him.

You can swear at the police all you choose to in Providence, Rhode Island, and there's little that can be done to stop you. Obscenities merely elicit feelings of "indignation, disgust or anger," and they are not considered to be "fighting words."

You can't get any kind of a drink, not even water, in Walden, New York, if you ask for it from someone who doesn't have a permit. The little community of Walden has an ordinance that prohibits citizens from giving a drink to another person without first acquiring a special license from the city fathers.

A man can ban his mother-in-law from his home without having any particular good reason in Iowa. And in Wichita, Kansas, a husband is allowed to mistreat his mother-in-law just as much as he pleases. His attitudes and actions cannot be used as divorce grounds.

In the quiet little community of Pateros, Washington, dogs are expressly forbidden to be a nuisance and get in the way of people walking on the streets. And in Tulsa, Oklahoma, dogs are prohibited from going on private property without first getting the owner's consent.

A hastily passed Indiana antipornography law prohibits any public performance of "excretory functions." The harried legislators realized too late that their broad wording had also outlawed such common things as coughing, sneezing, sweating, spitting, or even blowing one's nose.

The state of Washington has a commonsense law on how to decide the winner of an election in case of a tie in the vote count. It's simply done by the flipping of a coin by an official at the county courthouse in the presence of both candidates.

Speaking of ridiculous laws! The Missouri legislature really passed a winner. No one knows exactly what it is, what it means, or how it works. The title? Senate Substitute for Senate Committee Substitute for House Substitute for House Committee Substitute for House Bill 657. A brilliant piece of legislative tomfoolery, to say the least.

Yet the legislators of Virginia even topped this. They straightfacedly passed a statute in 1930 entitled: "To Prohibit Corrupt Practices or Bribery by Any Person Other Than Candidates."

The beautiful city of Mobile, Alabama, has an ordinance that outlaws any adult or child from bathing in a public drinking fountain in a city park. And in Seattle, Washington, it's against the law to use any water while there is a fire in the area. The statute makes no provision for simply taking a drink of water if you are thirsty.

Pasadena, California, forbids a secretary from ever being alone in an office with the boss!

One of Flowery Branch, Georgia's claims to fame is

this little-known piece of ludicrous legalese passed un-smilingly by the local politicos: *"Be it ordained, and it is hereby ordained, by the Mayor and Council of the Town . . . that on and after this date it shall be unlawful for any person or persons to hollar snake within the city limits of said town."*

Montana has made it a felony for a wife to open and read a telegram sent to her husband. Nothing in the law mentions a husband's doing the same thing to his wife's telegrams. He can be as nosy as he pleases, especially if he suspects her of having an affair. But, alas, the poor wife can't!

Seattle, Washington, outlines specific limitations on the length of any concealed weapon which may be carried by a person. How long can this concealed weapon be? No more than six feet.

Concealed weapons are still covered by a special piece of 1912 legislation in Pocatello, Idaho. The law clearly says: "The carrying of concealed weapons is forbidden, unless same are exhibited to public view."

In Memphis, Tennessee, the law declares that you can't give any of the pie you ordered in a restaurant to a friend, nor are you allowed to put the pie into a napkin and take it home for eating later as a snack. You must, by law, eat every bit of the pie before leaving the restaurant.

Postmen are well protected in Tennessee. An early statute states that: "Mail carriers prevented from delivering the mail on time by the carelessness or inattentiveness of ferry boat operators may recover double damages for any loss or injury sustained thereby."

If you would like to kick your wife out of bed, don't move to the little town of Lebanon, Virginia. Such an act is illegal in that particular community. You can't even do it when her feet are cold and she plants them squarely in the middle of your back.

Nebraska does not restrict its female population from using profanity when angry at a man. But it's against the law for a man to curse and swear in front of a woman.

In Kansas City, Missouri, a child is allowed to buy a shotgun, but is banned from purchasing a toy cap pistol. And Onalaska, Washington, has a law that says you can't give a cap pistol or any other kind of toy gun to anyone under the age of eighteen years if the toy pistol is going to be used for playing out-of-doors.

Kansas City, Kansas, still enforces an obscure 1901 statute regarding women caught on a city street late at night and alone. According to this law, women are subject to arrest if they are "in the streets or any public place without lawful business and without giving a good accounting of themselves."

Laughable Laws in
Foreign Places

A DRIVER CRUISING Leighton Buzzard, Great Britain, is not allowed to kiss a companion while driving on "winding roads." The driver can be fined an amount equal to forty-eight dollars, and his or her passenger can be fined one half that amount.

Even rock and roll music comes under the gun in Munich, Germany. A group of fun lovers who happen to enjoy playing together in a swimming pool, or wrestling in mud, can't partake of this activity if there is rock and roll music playing in the background. This loony law was decreed by Munich's Office for Public Order. The logic? This legislation was passed simply for "reasons of hygiene and the risk of sexual orgies." According to this law, by omission of course, it's fine to mud wrestle or have a wild pool party—if Willie Nelson if doing the singing!

Most people tend to think of the French Riviera as an absolute paradise for fun and games of an adult nature. But it's illegal for women there to bare their breasts on the beaches. Topless bathing suits are prohibited in public.

Nude sunbathing is closely regulated by the city council of Tropea, Italy. Such activities are allowed, but with specific important reservations. First of all, males are not legally able to appear unclothed on a public beach. Secondly, no women are allowed to appear nude on a local beach if they happen to be "fat, ugly, or generally unattractive." The law specifically says nude sunbathing can be undertaken only by "young women capable of exalting the beauty of the female body."

Palermo, Italy, allows nude sunbathing on a limited basis, according to the sex of the bather. Females can sunbathe nude in public places whenever the desire strikes. A man will be fined $10.00 for doing exactly the same thing! Why? Because the law states: "The male anatomical conformation can become obscene, even unconsciously."

It's against the law in Sweden for teenage girls to take full-length pictures of themselves in the nude—if the photographs are taken in a coin-operated photomat found in bus, subway, and train stations. Photos from the waist up in the nude are legal, as are nude photos of the girl from the waist down.

In Greece, a man cannot falsely promise to marry a girl in order to seduce her. If he does, and the woman has intercourse with him, the man must compensate her financially for the premarital loss of her virginity.

Also in Greece, in this case in Athens, you can lose your driver's license if you operate a motor vehicle on the public roads "poorly dressed" or "unbathed."

Port Moresby, New Guinea, has a law that regulates the legal prices to be paid for a wedding partner. *A man*

must pay five pigs, one bird, and $240 cash for a "brand-new bride." For a widower or a divorced woman it's two pigs, one bird and only a thirty-dollar fee. For a woman who has already been married twice, the law states: "Such women are of no commercial value."

A special law was passed in lovely little Micronesia which prohibits men from wearing neckties anywhere in the country. Why bother legislating such trivia? Because, as the law states, neckties have "absolutely no redeeming social qualities." The laughable law also contains specific penalties as it further declares: "Any citizen who chooses to wear a necktie in violation of this act shall be considered an idiot and upon conviction, shall have a piece of Yapese stone money tied around his neck for the duration of his natural life and thereafter until he mends his errant ways."

Men can be executed by a firing squad in Mogadishu, Somalia, if they get caught vocally opposing the law that gives equal rights to women. These men are convicted of "spreading propaganda" and of "undermining the government's authority."

Male visitors going to Uganda are not allowed to enter the country if they wear their hair long. The same is true in Saudi Arabia and Libya. Nor will authorities in Singapore tolerate long hair on men; there they pick up offenders and simply snip off the flowing locks. Tanzania has a variety of penalties for men with hair more than two inches in length and women wearing wigs or excessive makeup who are picked up on the streets. First offenders usually get just a warning, a haircut, and four "strokes with the cane." Second offenders can be sentenced to a jail term ranging anywhere from six months to life.

Uganda's bloodletting Marxist dictator, Idi Amin, passed all his laws by simple decree. He once became extremely concerned about the rampant venereal disease rate in his nation. The man felt that most citizens were embarrassed and would not readily seek medical help when finding they contracted such a disease. So how did Idi handle the situation? He renamed it, "Good Hope." Amin decreed the law in this manner: "From now on, all a person has to tell a doctor is 'Good Hope,' and he will be given treatment accordingly." One might wonder exactly what treatment he had in mind?

Don't try streaking while visiting Kenya! Under the "progressive legislation" of that African nation, their antistreaking law doesn't affect the local citizenry. Only foreign streakers are punished! What's the penalty for streaking in Kenya? The law is unmistakably clear: "Any foreign streaker will be immediately arrested, escorted directly to the airport in the nude and put aboard the first available aircraft to his country of origin." One question comes to mind. Since this ludicrous law specifically says "his," does it also apply to women who run down the streets in Kenya while naked?

In South Africa, after you are booked for drunk driving, it's automatically ten years in the penitentiary and/or a $2,800 fine.

Legislators in Johannesburg, South Africa, consider lovemaking to be a form of "popular entertainment," according to current law. Wives can, but husbands can't, charge their mate a fee for sexual favors. The law is quite specific! It declares that the wife should "take care" and try not to "overcharge" her husband. The reasoning? Because South African lawmakers consider the marriage bed to be "the poor man's opera."

In Malaysia the wife of a drunk driver is also penalized. She must go to jail with her spouse.

Under Turkish law the police are required to take a drunk driver twenty miles out into the countryside. He is then forced to walk back to town under the watchful eye of a police escort.

The Australians have a different method of handling this problem. They send the drunk driver's name to all of the local newspapers where it is published under the headline HE'S DRUNK AND IN JAIL.

Russia doesn't fool around with its drunk drivers. If a person is convicted of killing another person while operating a motor vehicle in a drunken state, the drunk driver can be executed by a firing squad.

Life behind the Iron Curtain can really be tough on men who decide to take on a second wife—without first going through a bothersome divorce proceeding. No man could possibly enjoy being convicted on a charge of bigamy in Communist-occupied Hungary! Current legislation would require the hapless husband to "live with both wives simultaneously, in the same house." Nothing in this unique piece of loony legalese covers bigamist women.

Bulgarian citizens with a sense of humor beware! Anyone who has the audacity to tell a joke about the Red dictatorship, and gets caught or reported, will receive a sentence of from two weeks to nine months in jail. And to think, the identical behavior in the United States often leads to television appearances and nightclub bookings!

And speaking of Communist-occupied Bulgaria, the authorities don't appear to take driving under the influence lightly! A second conviction will be the drunk driver's last. He will be executed!

In Lebanon all speed limit signs along the highways and roads must read: PROCEED MOST AWFULLY SLOWLY— 15 MILES TO THE HOUR.

A driving regulation in Tokyo, Japan, is translated for English-speaking drivers as: "When a passenger of the foot hoves into sight, tootie the horn trumpet. If he still obstacles your passage, tootie him with vigor and express by word of mouth warning, 'Hi Hi.' ''

Jaywalking is against the law in Swat, a tiny Himalayan state. Persons caught jaywalking are forced to run along the road until they fall over from total exhaustion.

Staid old England has some strange Sunday laws on the books regarding things a shopper can and cannot purchase at a store. Violation of the statute brings a twenty-five-pound fine for the shop owner. With regard to foodstuffs, you can't purchase canned milk, but buying fresh milk is all right. The purchase of other canned food is also illegal but that of any kind of horse feed is fine. If you want some tripe, it's only available raw. Cooked tripe is banned on the Sabbath. If you plan on eating out, you can buy fish *or* chips; you are not allowed to order fish *and* chips. Bars of soap can be purchased for bathing purposes, but boxes of soap for the laundry are outlawed.

In Great Britain, it's considered to be a "national nuisance" when a man tries to sell a vacuum cleaner to a woman in a public place. The salesman can be given a three-month jail sentence and a fine equalling one hundred and eighty dollars.

It's against the law in Heraklion, Crete, to write any profane words or suggestive sayings on a hotel room wall. Such an act is considered to be a "public insult" and punishable by nine months at hard labor.

Switzerland has a law that prohibits children under twelve years of age from riding in the front seat of a car. The only way around this statute is if the backseat is full, or if the vehicle has no backseat. In addition, the wearing of seat belts is mandatory in Switzerland for all adults, but not for kids. Any adult not making use of a seat belt is fined twenty francs. Swiss law also makes it mandatory for all visitors and citizens who wear glasses to carry an extra pair of glasses at all times when driving on a public road.

In Tanzania, women are prohibited from wearing miniskirts, tight-fitting dresses, and any kind of see-through clothing. Tight pants, western-style flared slacks, or bell-bottoms are banned for men. The penalty is a flogging.

Any male who fathers three children must by law be sterilized in Utar Pradish, a state in India. Men who refuse to do this voluntarily are imprisoned for a two-year period. Automatic sterilization is required while the penitentiary time is being served. Should the prisoner object to this procedure, he is to be castrated immediately.

According to the law in modern-day Egypt, belly dancers are prohibited from performing in public places unless their navel is covered with gauze. Does this imply that such women can legally dance in the nude so long as the belly button is hidden from view?

What is considered to be the serious crime of adultery in Abu Dhabi of the United Arab Emirates? A crime so bad it is always punishable by a death sentence? A man can be so charged for the simple act of kissing his lover on the cheek or forehead while in a public place. This illegal activity is considered to be ''committing an action that could be harmful to the general public.''

And in Korea, according to posted crossing signs, it is illegal to make love on (or do they simply mean to ''travel near'') railroad tracks. Decide for yourself. The railroad crossing signs read: POSITIVELY NO INTERCOURSE ON THESE TRACKS WHILE TRAINS ARE PASSING.

Jews in Great Britain are the only people allowed to keep their shops open on Sunday. In order to do this legally, the shop owner must be willing to close up on Saturday, the Jewish Sabbath, instead.

Prostitutes are rather well protected within the city limits of Bologna, Italy. The police are prohibited from taking away the driver's license of a female who gets caught dispensing her professional services in the back-seat of an automobile. This unique law states that a prostitute ''can drive a car carefully and at the same time lead a scandalous life.''

People living in Chile's Cautin province aren't allowed to keep pinups around the house. A decree issued by the military governor declares: ''It is more worthwhile to admire a good landscape than a photograph of a nude woman.''

Men in Bogota, Colombia, are protected by a special piece of loony legislation. They are legally entitled to shoot or otherwise kill ''an unfaithful spouse.'' But this is only true if the husband ''personally witnesses the corrupt activity'' while the sexual foray is actually in progress. The loving mate can't be prosecuted for murdering his adulterous wife. The retaliation he undertakes is by law said to be no more than ''an excusable act of passion.'' The female half of a marriage partnership is not entitled to do the same thing to her wayward hubby!

The North Yemen government issued the following ordinance: ''All official titles used in correspondence, addresses, mass media and in various official quarters will be completely abolished, to be replaced by the word 'brother' at all levels.'' The new statute was signed as follows: ''Lieutenant Colonel Ibahim Hamadi, Chairman of the Command Council and Commander in Chief of the Armed Forces.''

Additional Laws

Minnesota HAS A great law regarding state income tax filing. They are extremely thorough to say the least. The law requires taxpayers to include on their return their "name, address, Social Security number, age, date of birth, date of death."

Dogs in Smithtown, New York, can't bark for more than 15 minutes at a time. A first offense fine for prolonged barking is set at $50. A second offense brings $100, while a whopping $500 fine and a 15-day jail sentence are meted out for a third!

Cicero, Illinois, has a tough law dealing with snowfalls. When there happens to be three or more inches of snow in the city, a "street must be cleared of all vehicles or be towed away." Huh? It'd be amusing to watch a street being "towed away."

"A woman may not drive a car unaided," declares a law in Memphis, Tennessee. "A man must walk or run in front of the vehicle, waving a red flag in order to warn approaching pedestrians and motorists."

While in Pocatello, Idaho: "It is prohibited for pedestrians and motorists to display frowns, grimaces, scowls, threatening and glowering looks, gloomy and depressed facial appearances, generally all of which reflect unfavorably upon the city's reputation.''

Los Angeles County has a few new oddball laws which should have a tremendous impact on all their residents. No person can be caught taking his donkey for a stroll on the beach, nor can anyone graze cows or other livestock on the beach, in a park, or at other public places. No one is allowed to change clothes while at the arboretum, nor can vulgar language be used there. Nor can anyone launch a windsurfer on the wrong side of a county lake. The penalty for each of these? A $50 fine for the first offense in a year, $100 for a second and $250 for a third!

Birmingham, Alabama, offers this law from Section 135 of their City Ordinance: ''It shall be unlawful to drive within the corporate limits of the city a wagon or other vehicle drawn by goats for the purpose of advertising any article, trade, or occupation.''

Every month, according to a New York State law, theater owners are required to scrape the chewing gum from under their seats.

And in Columbus, Ohio, it's against the law to sell corn flakes on the Sabbath. Maybe Cheerios are okay?

Houston, Texas, goes one better in their ban on Sunday food purchases. They have outlawed the buying of limburger cheese, goose liver and rye bread on the Sabbath.

One-armed pianists may have trouble in Iowa if they expect to play before a full house. The law says ''a one-armed piano player may be seen, but not if admission is charged to view his performance.''

Florida isn't the place to live or visit if you enjoy taking baths. It's tough to get clean there. No one's allowed to bathe unless they're wearing a bathing suit or some other attire!

No self-respecting woman in Eureka, Kansas, can try to hatch pheasant eggs in a store.

Egyptian males certainly have little to complain about when it comes to getting proper respect in Cairo. The law there says that a female found guilty of cursing in the presence of a man will be put in jail for seven days. She'll get six months plus a fine if her crime is repeated within the same year.

Bermuda is a wonderful vacation spot, but tourists must be extremely careful while visiting. People are banned from walking around without shoes. Nor are short shorts or bathing suits suitable to wear in public places.

An old forgotten piece of loony legislation comes from England. Citizens who tried unsuccessfully to commit suicide weren't given a second chance. They were promptly hanged! But, then, Great Britain is also the country that recently passed a law exempting women with bust measurements of less than 32 inches from paying their 10 percent sales tax on dresses.

American tourists visiting Japan are given translations of local driving laws. Here are a few examples:

1. "Beware the wandering horse that he shall not take fright as you pass him by. Do not explode the gas box . . . go soothingly by."
2. "Go soothingly in the grease mud, as there lurks the skid demon."
3. "Give big space to the festive dog that shall sport in the roadway."